THE SHEPHERD'S CALENDAR

JOHN CLARE was born in the rural parish of Helpston, Northamptonshire, in 1793, the son of an agricultural labourer. For much of his life, he lived there and in the neighbouring village of Northborough. His first collection of poetry was the highly successful *Poems of Rural Life and Scenery* (1820), which was followed by *The Village Minstrel* (1821), *The Shepherd's Calendar* (1827) and *The Rural Muse* (1835). In 1837, after earlier periods of instability, he was admitted to High Beach asylum in Epping Forest, from which he escaped four years later, walking the ninety miles or so back to Northborough. Less than a year later, he was committed to the county asylum in Northampton, where he remained until his death in 1864. Throughout his life he wrote prolifically, composing well over three thousand poems, as well as much prose.

TIM CHILCOTT has maintained a lifetime interest in English Romantic literature, particularly the work of John Clare, about whom he has written extensively. His other major research interest is literary translation, and his website devoted to translation can be accessed at www.tclt.org.uk.

CARRY AKROYD is a painter and printmaker who has created many works inspired by John Clare's poetry. Her website is www.carryakroyd.co.uk.

Also by John Clare from Carcanet

A Champion for the Poor,
edited by P.M.S. Dawson, Eric Robinson and David Powell

John Clare by Himself,
edited by Eric Robinson and David Powell

Northborough Sonnets,
edited by Eric Robinson and David Powell

Cottage Tales,
edited by Eric Robinson, David Powell and P.M.S. Dawson

The Midsummer Cushion, edited by Anne Tibble

The Rural Muse, edited by R.K.R. Thornton

The Journals, Essays, and the Journey from Essex,
edited by Anne Tibble

John Clare

THE
SHEPHERD'S CALENDAR

MANUSCRIPT AND PUBLISHED VERSION

edited with an introduction by Tim Chilcott

with illustrations by Carry Akroyd

CARCANET

First published in Great Britain in 2006 by
Carcanet Press Limited
Alliance House
Cross Street
Manchester M2 7AQ

A CIP catalogue record for this book is available from the British Library
ISBN 1 85754 891 4
978 1 85754 891 4

The publisher acknowledges financial assistance from the
Margaret Grainger Fund and Arts Council England

Typeset in Palatino by XL Publishing Services, Tiverton
Printed and bound in England by SRP Ltd, Exeter

CONTENTS

LIST OF ILLUSTRATIONS

THE

SHEPHERD'S CALENDAR;

WITH

VILLAGE STORIES,

AND OTHER POEMS.

BY JOHN CLARE,

AUTHOR OF " POEMS ON RURAL LIFE AND SCENERY."—" THE
VILLAGE MINSTREL," &c.

LONDON:
PUBLISHED FOR JOHN TAYLOR, WATERLOO PLACE,
BY JAMES DUNCAN, PATERNOSTER ROW;
AND SOLD BY J. A. HESSEY, 93, FLEET STREET.
1827.

The title page of the 1827 edition of *The Shepherd's Calendar*

Introduction

This is a book that presents two versions of one of John Clare's most celebrated poems, *The Shepherd's Calendar*. Different versions of poems are, of course, nothing new in literary history. Clare's Romantic contemporaries provide notable examples of alternative texts: Wordsworth in his three distinct versions of *The Prelude*; Coleridge in the changes made to the first printed version of *The Ancient Mariner*, or *Frost at Midnight*, or *Dejection: An Ode*; Shelley in the differences between *Laon and Cythna* and *The Revolt of Islam*. Sometimes, such changes to poems come about from personal dissatisfaction with earlier versions; sometimes, in response to comment by friends, editors, publishers or critics; sometimes, both. On occasions, the changes are substantive; on others, more marginal. But whatever the cause and extent of the alterations, they indicate that poetic texts, far from being fixed and definitive, are often fluctuating and uncertain. How and why, then, did *The Shepherd's Calendar* come to exist in the two different versions presented here?

In 1819, Clare's work was first introduced to the London publisher, John Taylor; and one of the most striking features of their early correspondence is how immediately it focused upon specific literary concerns. Among Clare's manuscripts, Taylor had discovered 'a Plan' for a poem to be entitled 'A Week in a Village'; and in his very first letters to Clare, he at once suggested a detailed structure and organisation for the poem. Where the activities in the village were special to a particular day of the week, they could naturally be included under that day. The work, occupations, events and entertainments not selected in this way might then be divided among the remaining days of the week. A short piece of narrative, too, might be placed against the descriptive element in each day. If it were, a varied metric might be deployed to highlight the individual 'voice' of each narrator. Alternatively, some variety in stanzaic and metrical form might distinguish each particular day throughout. Overall, Taylor judged, diversity of form and treatment would allow Clare's distinctive poetic intelligence to be most fully realised:

'a varied Structure of Verse in a long Poem suits your Genius best.'[1]

The implications of this initial exchange were to reverberate for well over seven years, before *The Shepherd's Calendar, with Village Stories and other Poems* finally appeared in 1827. Although 'A Week in a Village' never advanced beyond a mere outline, it nevertheless anticipated questions about poetic structure and organisation that were to dominate the preparation of the later poem. The title itself – *The Shepherd's Calendar* – contained an obvious allusion to Edmund Spenser's sixteenth-century poem of the same name, which had been structured around the twelve months of the year. But if it seemed natural that Clare's poem should be similarly time-based, a question at once arose about what would provide the most effective temporal framework: the twelve months of the year, the four seasons, the seven days of the week, the twenty-four hours of day and night, or simply the hours of the waking day from dawn to nightfall? As a related structural issue, was the imaginative emphasis of the book to fall upon 'description', or upon 'narrative', or upon 'narratives' that were based upon 'description'? At different times, Clare, Taylor, and his publishing partner James Hessey, all seemed to have shared a view that some narrative element in the work would humanise and particularise what might otherwise be rather generalised descriptions of natural scenes. But the structural relationship between description and narrative, and then in turn between description, narrative and time, was less easily determined. If both descriptions and narratives were included, were the stories to be only loosely connected to the description (a story about Sunday games, say, simply because that is when they were played, or a tale about valentines in a description of February simply because of the calendar), or should the story issue from the evocation more closely and inevitably? If the latter strategy were adopted, however, what about tales that had no daily or monthly focus at all – that could have happened on Tuesday, Wednesday or Thursday, in June, July or August? And what about poems, especially, that might fall outside the categories of 'description' and 'narrative' altogether?[2]

These questions about the structural underpinning of the new poem were allied to others. As Clare began to send his drafts down to London, the distinctive qualities of his poetic intelligence soon became evident. This was a poetry of documentary energy and richness, where all the details of life in his native village of Helpston advanced into a democratic foreground of attention. It was verse of fullness and familiarity and self-sufficiency, crowded with flowers, animals, human figures, crops, weather, customs, which were known and accessible and authoritative. If it embraced a world – and an entire world at that – it was because at its centre lay an imaginative inclusiveness which, accepting everything, could then quite properly reject nothing. Such manifest strengths, though, did not come without a price. As detail followed detail in the manuscripts, the poetry began to risk sameness – a repetition not simply of work that had been published elsewhere (notably in the *London Magazine*, which Taylor edited between 1821 and 1825), but repetition even within individual pieces themselves. Against the plenitude and vigour of lived rural experience, both Taylor and Hessey began to voice significant words of a counterpoint: *select, refine, reflect, distil*. The mere catalogues of rural affairs, as they began to be seen, needed to be shaped and honed. Writing to Clare, Taylor presented what he saw as an important contrast in perception about the emerging poem: 'you wish to make it a complete Record of Country Affairs. I would have you only make a Selection of the Circumstances that will best tell in Poetry.'[3] Whereas Clare seemed to want to say everything, Taylor wanted him to say something.

If Taylor's antithesis addressed a significant literary tension between content and form (between a content that embraced fullness and communality, and a form that needed to fashion that fullness into poetic shape), it also pointed towards wider aspects of the public relationship between Clare and him: their position as poet and publisher, and the expectations that both had of their respective roles. As the drafts for the title-poem began to emerge, it is clear that Taylor offered much more than simply generalised approval of Clare's literary plans. Far from being merely the passive recipient of finalised manuscripts, Taylor was an active collaborator in their selection, revision, and even drafting. He criticised Clare's cataloguing yet suggested positive patterns of organisation, excised entire sections yet defended his distinctive style, damned one version of 'July' but warmly praised another, attacked slovenly handwriting and

composition yet spent hours doggedly transcribing nearly illeg-
ible drafts. It was a role that was at once both supportive and
critical, both dispassionate and interventionist.

How far this kind of close influence was arrogated by Taylor,
and how far willingly granted by Clare, is a question that
continues to generate very substantial debate. On one view,[4]
Taylor's responses have been construed as unnecessarily inva-
sive, even officious. His fundamental attitude, it has been
claimed, was both condescending and conservative. In moral
terms, the argument continues, he advanced a prudish, censo-
rious agenda by seeking to emasculate Clare's political
radicalism, as well as his sexual frankness. And in literary terms,
he time and again advocated that Clare should create work of
'significance' and 'sentiment' and 'elevation' – poetry of
contrived earnestness, in other words, so alien to Clare's natural
voice.

Undoubtedly, there are moments during the preparation of
The Shepherd's Calendar when Taylor's role as publisher takes on
a dominant, even dominating, cast. Unquestionably, too, there
are instances of irritation, even anger, between poet and
publisher, either (on Clare's part) because of the substantial
delays in publishing the volume, or (on Taylor's) because of the
inchoate state and quality of the manuscripts. But any neat view
of publisher as tyrant, and poet as victim, is based more in rhet-
oric than in evidence. What the testimony of some 180 letters
between Clare, Taylor, and Hessey shows – and fascinatingly so
– is the ambiguity of their respective roles, and the flexibility,
even hesitancy, with which each approached the process of
translating manuscript into print. Clare, for his part, clearly had
no view of his words as sacrosanct – tablets of stone that stood
as unalterable testament to the power of the poetic imagination.
His letters to Taylor are scattered with phrases like 'its your
liberty to make the best of em you can to select & throw aside
just as you please', 'your alterations…cannot be better[ed] so I
left them untouchd', 'you know better then me what will suit',
'I know you can make much better of [them] then I can', 'I send
them for you to do as you please with & finish the Poem in the
best manner that the materials alows you', 'you know better
when to publish the Vol…& I shall leave it wholly to you'.[5]
Taylor, for his part, equally clearly had no view of a publisher's

position as above the mundane job of copying out a barely decipherable manuscript in a fair hand.[6] He engaged in rudimentary editorial tasks of transcription and correction that were rarely, if ever, necessary with any of the firm's other writers. In fact, both Clare and Taylor ventured beyond inherited and conventional expectations, to confuse any neatly demarcated lines of power between poet and editor, or poet and publisher.

They did so, it may be argued, for a simple human reason. The relationship between them was not simply publicly or historically defined. It was also personal, and lived in a present tense. Being so, it was subject to all those blurrings of role, all the shifting uncertainties of need and response, that characterise actual experience. Different in personality though they were, their almost habitual modes of address and conclusion ('My dear Taylor...My dear Clare...ever sincerely yours...yours very sincerely...ever faithfully yours') suggest a simple liking for each other, on an instinctive level of personal affinity. Yet during the course of preparing *The Shepherd's Calendar*, both were ill, and seriously so. In the first months of 1824, Clare felt his 'insides sinking & dead', and his memory grown 'worse & worse nearly lost'. There was a sensation as if 'cold water was creeping all about [his] head', and a 'numbness all over',[7] for which the doctors could offer no diagnosis. Later that year, Taylor spent much of the autumn away from London, recuperating from a recurrent illness, only to collapse completely in August 1825 with an attack of 'brain-fever', from which there was scarcely any hope he would recover. How far such sickness was caused by constant pressure in both cases is not easy to determine. But neither was an idle man – indeed, the very reverse. Both overworked, did and wrote too much, seemed unable to resist or moderate the demands that were placed upon them. Both, too, had to deal with ambiguities of influence and responsibility, as they confronted aspects over which they had no control. If Clare frequently felt himself powerless over Taylor's delays, Taylor in turn seems to have been equally helpless in the face of delays by drawers and engravers, copyists and printers.[8]

What these and similar instances bring to life is the ordinary, even mundane, features of the poem's evolution, as well as the more momentous aspects of its language, or descriptive strength, or overall design. In October 1823, for example, Hessey wrote to Clare with important suggestions for particular descriptive and narrative features in each of the twelve months,[9] a number of which were finally adopted. In January 1826, Taylor damned the more than 500 lines of a draft for 'July', yet praised as 'very beautiful' sixteen lines that are unquestionably the most evocative and resonant in the entire month.[10] But against these significant instances stand many slower, more ponderous details: of, to take a single example, the drawn-out procedure whereby Clare sent his drafts down to London, which were then copied out fairly (though with omissions when words could not be read), which were then checked by Taylor and Hessey against the manuscript, which were then commented upon by them, which were then returned to Clare, which were then corrected or revised, which were then returned to London... It is a salutary reminder that the process of creating *The Shepherd's Calendar* was tedious as well as telling.

From the many interweaving details of the gestation, however, there eventually emerged in April 1827 the published book, *The Shepherd's Calendar, with Village Stories and other Poems*. And, as is now clear, the lengthy process of its birth had affected one crucial imaginative relationship. Clare had produced no single, definitive fair-copy of his title-poem, and the 'final' manuscript versions of each of the twelve months were scattered among some 400 pages of drafts and fragments, few of them dated or ordered. Not even this mass of material, though, made up the complete manuscript, for almost certainly, some intermediate stages of drafting and revision had been simply thrown away or otherwise lost. To compound the uncertainties, none of the 'press copy' – the material actually sent to the printers, and the subsequent galleys and proofs with corrections – has now survived, making it difficult, if not impossible, to determine who initiated or authorised any particular change (Clare alone, Taylor alone, Clare and Taylor in consultation, or others involved in the process such as Hessey and Harry Stoe Van Dyk). In the complexity, indeed, only one fact stands out incontrovertibly. Between Clare's 'final' manuscripts and the published version that his first readers saw, there were substantial differences. The manuscripts had not simply been translated into print; they had also been transformed.

The changes made to Clare's manuscripts can be divided into three major areas: alterations to grammatical features such as spelling, punctuation, and capitalisation; rearrangements of lines and stanzas into different sequences; and substantial cuts and omissions, sometimes of entire blocks in the original text.

The changes to spelling, punctuation and capitalisation may seem the slightest of these three differences, but they are also the most frequently occurring. Their impact is not dramatic or loud, but quietly persistent. Something of their continuous effect can be judged by placing the opening manuscript lines of 'August' beside their published form:

Harvest approaches with its busy day	HARVEST approaches with its busy day;
The wheat tans brown & barley bleaches barley grey	The wheat tans brown, and bleaches grey;
In yellow garb the oat land intervenes	In yellow garb the oatland intervenes,
& tawney glooms the valley thronged with beans	And tawny glooms the valley throng'd with beans.
Silent the village grows wood wandering dreams	Silent the village grows, – wood-wandering dreams
Seem not so lonely as its quiet seems	Seem not so lonely as its quiet seems;
Doors are shut up as on a winters day	Doors are shut up as on a winter's day,
& not a child about them lies at play	And not a child about them lies at play;
The dust that winnows neath the breezes feet	The dust that winnows 'neath the breeze's feet
Is all that stirs about the silent street	Is all that stirs about the silent street:
Fancy might think that desert spreading fear	Fancy might think that desert-spreading Fear
Had whisperd terrors into quiets ear	Had whisper'd terrors into Quiet's ear,
Or plundering armys past the place had come	Or plundering armies past the place had come
& drove the lost inhabitants from home	And drove the lost inhabitants from home.
The fields now claim them where a motley crew	The fields now claim them, where a motley crew
Of old & young their daily tasks pursue	Of old and young their daily tasks pursue.

The strengths and limitations in these two versions are characteristic of the poem as a whole. To the trained Clare reader, the complete absence of punctuation in the left-hand manuscript version (together with the use of ampersands and the occasional spelling variant) can evoke a powerful sense of natural, easy, unforced utterance. This is a seemingly artless, uncontrived language, where every detail is given equal syntactic weight, without any subordination or shaping by the signals of commas, colons, semi-colons, or full stops. The wheat, the barley, the oat land, the valley, the beans, the village – all advance equally into a foreground of capacious and democratic attention. But the rich simultaneity of reference that results is bought at a price. Rhythmic effects of pause or flow, of strong end-rhyme or run-on line, are uncertainly realised – to the extent of one couplet needing at least one rereading before its syntactic relationships become clear ('Silent the village grows wood wandering dreams / Seem not so lonely as its quiet seems'). It is this rhythmic and syntactic clarity, though, that the published version provides. The comma and dash after 'Silent the village grows, – ' clearly indicate the crucial medial caesura in the line, just as the hyphen in 'desert-spreading' signals a cojoined adjective. To modern taste, almost certainly, the effectiveness of capitalising the personifications ('Fear', 'Quiet') is more debatable; but the words are at least established *as* personifications, to be given an appropriate rhythmic stress that might well have been over-looked in the manuscript version.

The gains and losses specific to this extract are repeated throughout the poem. In grammatical terms, Clare's unpunctu-ated manuscripts, with their variants in spelling, convey to a modern eye a sense of untutored but vigorous individuality.[11] The published version, with its normalised spelling and punc-tuation, and logically applied verse paragraphing, conveys a sense of tutored yet intelligible clarity. And the notion of clarity – with associated terms such as 'coherence', 'connectedness', 'imaginative logic' – significantly informs the second area of difference between manuscript and printed text: the re-sequencing of material. One of the best examples of Taylor's changes in this respect occurs in 'February'.[12] Halfway through his evocation of the month, Clare presented these stanzas in his manuscript. They are in the first instance worth reading 'raw', without any introductory comment, so that their impact is unmediated:

> The gossips saunter in the sun
> As at the spring from door to door
> Of matters in the village done
> & secret newsings mutterd oer
> Young girls when they each other meet
> Will stand their tales of love to tell
> While going on errands down the street
> Or fetching water from the well
>
> A calm of pleasure listens round
> & almost whispers winter bye
> While fancy dreams of summer sounds

> & quiet rapture fills the eye
> The sun beams on the hedges lye
> The south wind murmurs summer soft
> & maids hang out white cloaths to dry
> Around the eldern skirted croft
>
> Each barns green thatch reeks in the sun
> Its mate the happy sparrow calls
> & as nest building spring begun
> Peeps in the holes about the walls
> The wren a sunny side the stack
> Wi short tail ever on the strunt
> Cockd gadding up above his back
> Again for dancing gnats will hunt

The generous plenitude of detail in these lines is unquestionable; but the shape of those details is more uncertain. An imaginative gear-change between first and second stanzas, and then between second and third, is fairly audible, and raises several questions. How, for instance, does 'fetching water from the well' connect to the immediately following 'calm of pleasure'? How does the rapturous dreaming of the second stanza relate to the reeking thatch, or sparrow's call, of the third? To compare the final lines of 'February' in manuscript and published versions, however, is to appreciate how skilfully transitions were fashioned out of abruptness, and evolution out of incongruity:

& oft dame stops her burring wheel	And oft Dame stops her buzzing wheel
To hear the robins note once more	To hear the robin's note once more,
That tutles while he pecks his meal	Who tootles while he pecks his meal
From sweet-briar hips beside the door	From sweet-briar hips beside the door.
The hedghog from its hollow root	The sunbeams on the hedges lie,
Sees the wood moss clear of snow	The south wind murmurs summer soft;
& hunts each hedge for fallen fruit	The maids hang out white clothes to dry
Crab hip & winter bitten sloe	Around the elder-skirted croft:
& oft when checkd by sudden fears	A calm of pleasure listens round,
As shepherd dog his haunt espies	And almost whispers Winter by;
He rolls up in a ball of spears	While Fancy dreams of Summer's sound,
& all his barking rage defies	And quiet rapture fills the eye.
Thus nature of the spring will dream	Thus Nature of the Spring will dream
While south winds thaw but soon again	While south winds thaw; but soon again
Frost breaths upon the stiffening stream	Frost breathes upon the stiff'ning stream,

& numbs it into ice – the plain	And numbs it into ice: the plain
Soon wears its mourning garb of white	Soon wears its mourning garb of white;
& icicles that fret at noon	And icicles, that fret at noon,
Will eke their icy tails at night	Will eke their icy tails at night
Beneath the chilly stars & moon	Beneath the chilly stars and moon.
Nature soon sickens of her joys	Nature soon sickens of her joys,
& all is sad & dumb again	And all is sad and dumb again,
Save merry shouts of sliding boys	Save merry shouts of sliding boys
Bout the frozen furrowd plain	About the frozen furrow'd plain.
The foddering boy forgets his song	The foddering-boy forgets his song,
& silent goes wi folded arms	And silent goes with folded arms;
& croodling shepherds bend along	And croodling shepherds bend along,
Crouching to the whizzing storms	Crouching to the whizzing storms.

Not only are the incongruous lines about the hedgehog replaced by the now much more consonant stanza evoking rapturous quietness, but an even firmer transition is created by reversing the original order of the two quatrains. 'A calm of pleasure' followed by 'The sun beams' becomes 'The sunbeams' followed by 'A calm of pleasure'. As a result, the murmuring of the south wind now leads naturally into the listening 'calm of pleasure'; the dreams of summer's sounds fluently anticipate the subsequent dreams of Nature for the spring. What the re-sequencing has achieved is an effortless transition over a large imaginative space: from the naturalistic detail of the dame's spinning wheel and the robin's song, to the almost phantasmal landscape of the 'croodling shepherds… / Crouching to the whizzing storms'.

The conclusion to 'February' is not the only example of a reordering that achieves a new fluency of imaginative relationship. Similar changes to the two sections of 'January', to the end of 'October', to the stanzaic connections in 'November', and to the final lines of 'December', all enhance the poetic coherence of Clare's evocation. But if such reorganisation of existing material conferred clear benefits, the third area of change between manuscript and published version proved far more contentious. The 'final' manuscript versions that Clare sent to Taylor contained a total of 2,795 lines. The published text when it appeared contained 1,913. Almost a third of the poem had been cut.

It has long been argued[13] that three features in the poem were especially subject to Taylor's blue pencil: Clare's use of dialect, his expressions of political radicalism, and his earthy description of sensual pleasures. It is worth quantifying, first of all, the basic data for these three aspects.

Dialect words: although the definition of 'dialect word' is not incontrovertible, between 40 and 45 occurrences of such terms ('mawl', 'struttle', 'motling', 'slive', and so forth) occur in the manuscripts, but not in the printed text. It is worth noting, however, that many of them appear in much longer passages that have been excised (i.e. relatively few dialect terms seem to have been excised *purely and exclusively* because they were 'provincialisms'). Moreover, some 35-40 dialect occurrences remain in the published version ('crizzling', 'sliveth', 'croodling', 'hings', 'moiling', 'younker', and so on). The proportion of dialect words excised amounts to approximately 0.2% of the total number of words in the 'final' manuscript version.

Political radicalism: lines explicitly attacking enclosure ('May', 459-60), the differences between rich and poor ('June', 165-8), and the tyranny of justice ('October', 45-6) are clearly deleted; but they amount to eight lines only, less than 0.5% of the 'final' manuscript.

'Indelicacies': couplets describing physical features (sweating ploughmen, bottles of ale, blistered skin and corns on the feet, as well as girls' breasts) are equally clearly excised; but again, they comprise less than 0.75% of the total lines in the manuscript.

Quantity, of course, is not quality – and the minute percentages above could well belie a much larger imaginative emasculation. Self-evidently, the deletion of a dialect word like 'sturting' or 'mozzld' or 'soodling' will have a far greater impact upon a line than the omission of more neutral terms like 'field' or 'cow' or 'sun' or 'the'. But these tiny percentages could not belie emasculation to the extent that has been argued by some commentators. The fact remains that, in quantitative terms at least, scarcely 1.5% of the text *actually* excised by Taylor seems to have been cut for the reasons adduced by his critics.

Why apparently marginal causes should have been placed at the centre of argument, and the centre marginalised, is not hard

to understand. For over a generation, the prevailing interpreta-
tion of Clare's relationship with Taylor has been sharply
politicised, with Clare perceived as working-class victim at the
mercy of bully-boy patrons and capitalist publishers. But the
overwhelming evidence suggests that Clare's drafts were cut, not
for political but for far more obvious literary reasons. They were
sometimes demonstrably too long, and where they were, the
impact of his evocation was attenuated rather than concentrated.
In Taylor's strenuously expressed view, the first draft of 'July',
which ran to over 500 lines before turning into another poem alto-
gether, was a 'descriptive Catalogue in *rhyming Prose* of all the
Occupations of the Village People, scarcely one Feature of which
has not been better pictured before by you'.[14] The two sections of
'January', too, comprised well over 500 lines, causing further
concern about length. And in 'May', which ran to some 470 lines,
a clear hostage to fortune was offered in the admission that

> My wild field catalogue of flowers
> Grows in my ryhmes as thick as showers
> Tedious & long as they may be
> To some they never weary me

(193–6)

With prolixity came associated concerns: catalogues of flowers,
or plants, or birds, or animals, that generously reached out to
capture a whole world, but that did so at the expense of imagi-
native shaping and design. There were any number of
powerfully realised descriptions that could still be temporarily
interrupted by an incongruous detail, or actual redundancy. It
is significant that the three shortest months in Clare's manu-
scripts ('October' [120 lines], 'December' [152], and 'February'
[160]) were cut on average by less than a fifth. The three longest
('May' [470 lines], 'January' [558], and the first version of 'July'
[714]) were cut on average by over a half. Far more than dialect
words, or brief political references, or supposed 'indelicacies',
the sheer length of the poem brought about what may be
deemed a necessary contraction.

'Necessary contraction' is not a phrase that has often been
applied to Clare's drafts of *The Shepherd's Calendar*, and for
reasons that have already been mentioned. Viewed simply as a

social and historical document – which has frequently been the case – the poem could scarcely be long enough. Detail after detail provides an extraordinary sense of rootedness, of what it was like to live at that time and in that place. The details yield facts, information, feelings, attitudes, that are embedded in the specific, lived experience of Helpston in the 1820s. Consider for instance the following passage from the manuscript of 'January':

> On corner walls a glittering row
> Hang fire irons less for use then show
> Tongues bright wi huswifes rubbing toil
> Whod sooner burn her hands then soil
> When sticks want mending up & when
> Mores sought to eke the blaze agen
> & sifter dangling by their side
> & poker in the fire untryd
> & horshoe brightend as a spell
> Witchcrafts evil powers to quell
> & warming pan reflecting bright
> The crackling blazes twittering light
> That hangs the corner wall to grace
> & seldom taken from its place
> Save when the winter keener falls
> Searching thro the cottage walls
> Then quaking from the cottage fire
> Warm beds as comforts they require
> Yet still tis bright as gold can be
> & childern often peep to see
> Their laughing faces as they pass
> Gleam on the lid as plain as glass

The ostensible focus of these twenty-two lines – how they begin and end, at least – is the play of light upon the fire-irons that hang on the cottage wall. But much else is also introduced. The 'huswife's' role and attitude, both towards polishing the irons and towards rearranging or adding to the wood on the fire, are mentioned and elaborated. The details of a shovel and unused poker are noted. When the winter cold is especially severe, it can be felt permeating the walls of the cottage. Although the fire-irons may be more for display than actual use, the warming pan is nevertheless taken upstairs to bed when it is particularly cold. And these various pieces of additional information are expressed in words that are rooted in vibrant, localised speech and accent: tongues (tongs), wi (with), huswifes (housewife's), then (than), eke (increase), agen (again), sifter (shovel).

The published version of these lines, however, reads differently:

> On corner walls, a glittering row,
> Hang fire-irons – less for use than show;
> With horse-shoe brighten'd, as a spell,
> Witchcraft's evil powers to quell;
> And warming-pan, reflecting bright
> The crackling blazes' flickering light,
> That hangs the corner wall to grace,
> Nor oft is taken from its place:
> There in its mirror, bright as gold,
> The children peep, and straight behold
> Their laughing faces, whilst they pass,
> Gleam on the lid as plain as glass –

The original twenty-two lines have been reduced to twelve, and changes made to both individual words and accidentals. But importantly, the lines now concentrate almost wholly upon the single theme of light, and how it plays on the fire-irons. The discursive interpolation of other issues (the housewife, the adding or rearranging of wood, the winter cold, and so on) is excised in favour of a single imaginative focus: light on metal. Whereas the thrust in the manuscript version is centrifugal, outwards towards any number of things, the thrust in the published version is centripetal, inwards towards one thing alone.

If this and similar examples constitute 'necessary contraction', they do so for a simple reason. To recall Taylor's contrast,[15] *The Shepherd's Calendar* is not simply historical record or sociological report. It is also – and crucially so – a poem. As such, its documentary fullness or historical insights stand at best alongside (and many might argue, well behind) its imaginative persuasiveness, the tension and force of its verbal utterance. And poetic utterance concentrates. Few if any poems in literary history have ever suffered by being made shorter. And in this regard, the published version of the poem was far from a violation of Clare's manuscripts. In many ways, indeed, it supported and enhanced them.

Underlying this debate between manuscript and published version are important theoretical issues about the nature of Clare's text, and about what should stand at the centre of editions of his work. It has been argued, at one extreme, that the only legitimate centre is the manuscripts themselves, and the retrieval and presentation of them as closely as possible to their original, 'unmediated' form. All else is secondary, if not actually extraneous and irrelevant. From this point of view, the centre of this edition is nothing more than the verso pages of manuscript transcription. Indeed, even these can be only a printed approximation to the living individuality of Clare's hand, in the process of writing each new word and line and stanza. At the other extreme, however, the only legitimate centre is the poem and the entire context that surrounds it – not simply the relationship between manuscript and printed text, but those countless interlocking webs of personality and relationship, written and spoken exchange, words and deeds, creativity and the balance sheet, politics and the price of paper. Some aspects in this complex evolution are naturally more significant than others, but everything in the making of *The Shepherd's Calendar* potentially matters, and counts. The centre of this edition, in other words, is nothing less than everything it contains – and unquestionably a great deal more.

Whatever position individual readers of *The Shepherd's Calendar* may take in this discussion, a simple glance across from left- to right-hand pages in this book will show the results of the debate. The verso pages present the 'final' manuscript version of each month, with an indication of the *probable* period between first draft and last revision.[16] Individual variants in the nearly 400 pages of drafts that precede this 'final' version are summarised in *SC* (1996 [OET]), 3–162 (see Sources, Abbreviations and Further Reading, below). On these left-hand pages, all of Clare's solecisms are retained, together with his habitual use of the ampersand, and of double rather than single quotation marks. The only change made, in common with current editorial practice, has been to leave a space between those contractions of pronoun and verb that might be confused with other words (I'll, he'll, she'd, for example, which Clare would write as Ill, hell, shed, consequently read I ll, he ll, she d).

The recto pages of this edition, the 1827 published version that finally emerged, are then presented against the manuscript reading line for line. Since a good deal of the manuscript was cut, there are inevitably blank spaces (sometimes extending over several pages) wherever the excisions occur. It is very important, however, to read the recto pages as a visually coherent unity, without any breaks at all, since that is naturally the way the poem appeared on the published page in 1827. The eye, in other words, should move from the beginning to the end of a break as quickly as possible.

Although a few pre-publication copies of *The Shepherd's Calendar, with Village Stories, and Other Poems* were available in November 1826, it was only in April 1827 that the completed volume, prefaced by a drawing of an August harvest scene by Peter de Wint, was published (see opposite). Running to some 240 pages, of which *The Shepherd's Calendar* itself comprised the first hundred, the book was well produced, with the text set cleanly on the page, and surrounded by generous, proportionate margins. De Wint's engraving was in Clare's view 'a very beautiful thing…done uncommonly well',[17] and attractive enough to promote good sales. Yet almost immediately upon publication, there were ominous signs of a disappointing reception. In terms of the reviews, both the *Eclectic Review* and the *Literary Chronicle* warmly praised the new volume, the former particularly commending the imaginative growth it embodied.[18] But other reviews were more mixed; and two were openly hostile to the dialect expressions they found.[19] In different circumstances, such a range of response might have led to a richly orchestrated literary battle: dialect supporters versus dialect detractors, political radicals versus political conservatives. But the final impression generated by the reviews is not of sharply energised positions, but of fitful, even desultory response. Five or six reviews, and then nothing. The impact of a much wider world was beginning to make itself felt.

That world seemed more and more caught up by major economic and political concerns. Over a year before the poem's publication, Taylor had written to Clare with a gloomy account of city affairs: 'Business is very flat indeed in London. Nothing is doing…'. A general slump in trade, and some dramatic publishing bankruptcies in particular,[20] moved to the centre of the

Engraving from Peter De Wint's drawing of a scene from 'August'

London literary scene; and although the recession seems not to have affected the number of books published, Clare's volume was only one of some 1,000 or more books brought out in 1827, many of which spoke to the reading public's invincible sentimentalism, or piety, or desire for scandal, or interest in 'useful knowledge'. Literature became prettified into a tinsel world of keepsakes and annuals and cheap, fashionable novels – or alternatively became the disciplined rod of the expanding machine-age. More and more, too, fundamental issues of political reform were beginning to shape a national psyche, as the country slowly edged towards the formation and passing of the Great Reform Bill of 1832. For Fanny Kemble, society was becoming 'a sort of battlefield, for every man (and every woman too) is nothing if not political'.[21] And the *Athenaeum* commented: 'in truth, till the great question of reform is settled, we need look for no commanding works in either literature or art...the great market of literature will not open its gates full and wide, till the public mind is settled...'.[22]

It is easy to underestimate the impact of this wider economic and political context upon the reception of *The Shepherd's Calendar*. But in fact, the context powerfully influenced the reading public's response. Had the book appeared within a year or so of Clare's second volume, *The Village Minstrel* (1821), it might still perhaps have ridden on the wave of a continuing interest in 'rural poetry'. But that wave was already slowing; and there is no evidence to suggest that, had *The Shepherd's Calendar* come out in April 1824 or April 1825, its reception would have been markedly different from what it was two years later. Indeed, a single event, which Clare himself witnessed in July 1824 and which deeply moved him,[23] seems to have marked not only a symbolic but also an actual turning moment – away from poetry and the life of the imagination towards the practical, the mechanical, the utilitarian. With the death of Byron and the passing of his funeral cortège through the streets of London, a world and a culture quite simply changed. Contemporaries recalled hearing the news of his death with a clarity and precision that marked a shattering, momentous event.[24] In Bulwer Lytton's words, 'when Byron passed away, the feeling he had represented craved utterance no more. With a sigh we turned to the actual and practical career of life: we awoke from the morbid, the passionate, the dreaming...'.[25]

By mid-1829, more than two years after its publication, *The Shepherd's Calendar* had sold only 425 copies of what had probably been an edition of 1,000; and Clare's subsequent attempts to sell the remaindered books around Helpston met with little success. 1832 seems the last year in which the book was noted at all, when selected passages from each of the months appeared in William Hone's *The Year Book*.[26] To all intents and purposes, the title-poem and accompanying material then disappeared as a text for over a century and a quarter. Only in 1964 did the manuscript version of the full title-poem emerge again, in a ground-breaking edition by Eric Robinson and Geoffrey Summerfield that did much to resurrect Clare's reputation. Even this, though, seems to have sold steadily rather than spectacularly, with annual sales, on average, of fewer than 200 copies.[27] A second edition appeared in 1993, with a scholarly version of the manuscripts in 1996. A facsimile of the 1827 volume, meanwhile, came out in 1991. It is only now, however, some 180 years after the poem's first appearance, that its two principal versions can be seen side by side, in a parallel text.

What that parallel text may begin to suggest is that the areas of imaginative commonality between manuscript and published version are far more substantial than the areas of difference. Both versions present, for instance, numerous passages where the atmospheric resonance of the month or the landscape is especially heightened. The icy scenes and slow flights of birds in 'January' and 'February', the hail-storm and solitary crane of 'March', the blistering, claustrophobic heat of a July noonday, the winds and skyscapes of 'October' and 'November' – all these episodes, and many comparable scenes, are tellingly present in both versions. But the commonality goes beyond individual scenes. Both versions of *The Shepherd's Calendar* present a poem that is charged with a central theme: the relationship between natural and human cycles of time.

Any poetic portrayal of human and natural worlds through the perspective of time – whether of seasons or months, weeks or days – speaks to a tradition with ancient roots. The tradition goes back at the very least to Greek and Roman literature (Hesiod, Theocritus, Virgil), and almost certainly beyond that, into pre-literate times. His own native inheritance, too, provided Clare with countless illustrations of poetry based upon motifs of duration and temporal process. From the sixteenth-century example from which he had derived his title (Spenser's *Shepheardes Calendar*, 1579), through texts in the next century like Giles Fletcher's *Piscatorie Eclogs* (1633), to numerous works by eighteenth-century writers (Pope's *Pastorals*, Gay's *Shepherd's Week*, Ramsay's *The Gentle Shepherd*), there was a wealth of poetry evoking human and natural scenes conditioned by time. Significantly, the first poem to capture Clare's imagination as a boy was James Thomson's *The Seasons* (1730), a central exploration of the relationships between landscape and process, space and time.

The host of imitations that followed Thomson's model in the later eighteenth century and on into the nineteenth is some indication of both its attractiveness and its accessibility. Thematically, such imitations tapped into a basic, instinctual reservoir of response towards growth, fruition and decay, in both human and natural terms. Structurally, they provided an immediately recognisable poetic shape: the natural phases of spring, summer, autumn, winter; or morning, afternoon, evening, night. Even when the divisions of time chosen by writers were more obviously culturally determined (the days of the week, or months of the year), the appeal remained to a fundamental rhythm and pattern in the world's affairs.

But although *The Shepherd's Calendar* clearly works within a tradition that has widespread currency, it equally addresses newly emerging perceptions about the relationship between natural and human time. In one of the seminal modern explorations of how the nature of time has been portrayed in literature, the French critic Georges Poulet argues that the century into which Clare was born witnessed the emergence of a major literary theme:

> The great discovery of the eighteenth century is the phenomenon of memory. By remembering, man escapes the purely momentary; by remembering, he escapes the nothingness that lies in wait for him between moments of existence. ... To exist...is to be one's present, and also to be one's past and one's recollections.[28]

The effect of this new understanding is to erode earlier certainties of the relationship between natural and human time.

Whereas past portrayals presented natural and human time as consonant, parallel and intelligible (we are born, live and die, just as nature is born, lives and dies), now the phenomenon of time is no longer securely exteriorised in nature – in the ancient rhythms of day and night, or spring, summer, autumn and winter. Time has also become internalised – into a diffused, complex amalgam of individual perceptions about past, present and future, about memory and memorialising, about personal loss and gain through time. And in that internalisation, the old ties between natural and human time begin to be dissolved.

The Shepherd's Calendar does not present this dissolving as either dramatic or completed. But at a number of moments in both versions of the poem, Clare evokes a human world that is different, even estranged, from natural rhythms. That the opening of 'January' or the conclusion to 'December' should present human figures huddling against the cold of winter is not surprising. But in 'July', the summer heat is no less oppressive. In 'April', children picking violets irresistibly bring to mind the stark human contrast between childhood and maturity. The riot of flowers in the later part of 'June' concludes, numbingly, with a lost social cohesion: 'all this is past'. And 'May' explicitly presents the difference between natural things and human perception: 'in sweet natures holiday / His heart is sad while all is gay'. What these and similar examples evoke is the growing distance for Clare between natural and human time. For all its cyclic certainties, natural time operates as purest neutrality, a-social, a-moral, a-spiritual. Human time, however, is haunted by memory and by loss, and by what for him was to become an increasingly unbridgeable chasm between past and present.

In many ways, *The Shepherd's Calendar* is a poem poised on the cusp between these two perceptions of time: the dispassionate securities of natural time against the passionate uncertainties of human time. And the tension between these different perceptions helps to explain why the tone of voice sounded in *The Shepherd's Calendar* is, ultimately, both celebratory and elegiac. The inexhaustible fullness and presentness and self-sufficiency of things – their known place in the rhythms of natural time – are celebrated in an almanac of rare fidelity and persuasiveness, one of the richest and most eloquent expressions of English rural life, in the nineteenth or any other century. But things also fall apart; and as those things – landscapes, customs, human figures, feelings – begin to fracture in the whirl and flux of personal time, so Clare also memorialises them, to try and stave them from the irrevocable flow of time into a vanished Eden.

Tim Chilcott
April 2006

ACKNOWLEDGEMENTS

Like any student of Clare, I owe thanks to all those editors, keepers and interpreters of his work who have secured such firm foundations to support new inquiry. The editors of the Oxford English Texts (OET) edition of Clare, Eric Robinson, David Powell, and Paul Dawson, have worked for many years to produce a monumental edition, completed in 2003; and I am greatly indebted to all their skills of decipherment and scrupulous transcription. The late Geoffrey Summerfield, also, deserves a special mention for his major contribution to the editing of Clare's work. I thank, too, Glenys Wass of Peterborough Museum, and Juliette Baxter and Terry Bracher of Northampton Museum and Art Gallery, for their assistance, and Celia Coates of Nottingham Trent University for facilitating the loan of microfilms of Clare's manuscripts. I am particularly grateful to three long-standing members of the Clare community who have read parts of my text, and who have given such valuable and incisive advice. To Paul Dawson, John Goodridge, and Bob Heyes, my warmest appreciation. Elsewhere, three other central members of the Clare Society, Ronald Blythe, Paul Chirico and Peter Moyse, have offered kindly guidance; and Paul Foster and the Margaret Grainger Trust have made a generous contribution towards production costs. In the later stages of preparing the edition, it has been a pleasure to acknowledge the art of Carry Akroyd, whose illustrations so enhance the text, and the support of Judith Willson at Carcanet Press, who has been an exemplary editor.

There is an ultimate acknowledgement, of course, that stretches back over almost two centuries. To John Clare, and to his first editors John Taylor and James Augustus Hessey, a simple yet momentous thank you. But for you, this book would not exist.

Tim Chilcott

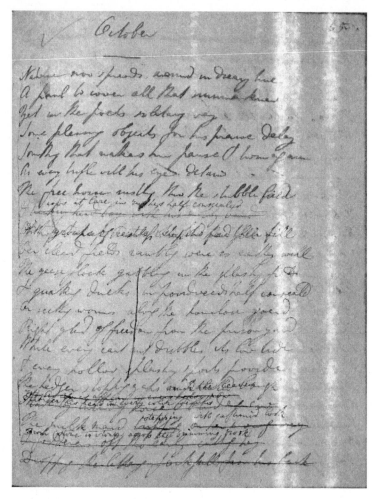

A characteristic page of Clare's manuscript: the opening lines of 'October'. Reproduced by kind permission of Peterborough Museum and Art Gallery

(*opposite*) A characteristic double-page spread from the 1827 edition of *The Shepherd's Calendar*: the end of 'September' and the opening of 'October'

Where time hath many seasons won,
Since aught beneath them saw the sun ;
Within these brambly solitudes,
The ragged, noisy boy intrudes,
To gather nuts, that, ripe and brown,
As soon as shook will patter down.

Thus harvest ends its busy reign,
And leaves the fields their peace again ;
Where Autumn's shadows idly muse
And tinge the trees in many hues :
Amid whose scenes I'm fain to dwell,
And sing of what I love so well.
But hollow winds, and tumbling floods,
And humming showers, and moaning woods,
All startle into sudden strife,
And wake a mighty lay to life ;
Making, amid their strains divine,
Unheard a song so mean as mine.

OCTOBER.

———

NATURE now spreads around, in dreary hue,
A pall to cover all that summer knew ;
Yet, in the poet's solitary way,
Some pleasing objects for his praise delay ;
Something that makes him pause and turn again,
As every trifle will his eye detain :—
The free horse rustling through the stubble field ;
And cows at lair in rushes, half conceal'd ;
With groups of restless sheep who feed their fill,
O'er clear'd fields rambling wheresoe'er they will ;
The hedger stopping gaps, amid the leaves,
Which time, o'er-head, in every colour weaves ;
The milkmaid pausing with a timid look,
From stone to stone, across the brimming brook ;

THE
SHEPHERD'S CALENDAR

Verso pages present the 'final' manuscript version.
Recto pages present the 1827 published version.

DEDICATION [1]

[15 July 1826]

I have often tryed at a Dedication for him [the Marquis of Exeter]
& cannot get one to my mind   I want one simply honest & out
of the beaten track of fulsome dedications one very short & very
plain & I think if I set it down here in my own way you will soon
make one out by it properly in your own   I want somthing in
this way   I expect I must call him noble – To the Most Noble
the Marquis of Exeter these Poems are Dedicated in remem-
brance of unmerrited kindness by his Lordships faithful servant
the Author" or "John Clare" as you please – I dont like to puff
nor I dont like to flatter so if you dont like it put a simple straight
forward thing down in your own way

DEDICATION

1827

TO

THE MOST NOBLE

THE MARQUIS OF EXETER,

IN GRATEFUL REMEMBRANCE OF

UNMERITED FAVOURS,

THESE POEMS

ARE, WITH PERMISSION,

MOST RESPECTFULLY INSCRIBED,

BY HIS LORDSHIP'S FAITHFUL

AND DEVOTED SERVANT,

THE AUTHOR.

PREFACE [2]

[after 5 September 1826]

Prefaces are such customary things, & so often repeated that I think good ones cannot always be expected or looked for by their readers & I am happy that they are so for it gives me an opper-tunity of saying somthing which I am anxious to say & at the same time leaves me the hope that I shall be pardoned for saying it so ill.

I feel desirous to return thanks to my friends who I am happy to say are too numerous to speak of here in any other then a general manner   yet I should be doing an injustice to my feel-ings if I were not to mention the honourable testimony of friendship received from Sir Michael Clare of the West Indies whose kind notice was as unlooked for as it was gratifying   & though it may be considered a species of vanity to be elated at such things I feel proud to confess that I am. Nor can I pass by the kind assistance afforded me by an early literary friend who first ushered my Poems into notice & still corrects them for publication   to his critical abilitys I owe a great portion of my success & surely such deeds should not pass without acknowl-edgments when they can be repaid so easily   & I feel some reluctance in leaving my catalogue unfinished but however the praises of friends may gratify ones self whom they a[re f]elt they may gratify the reader but little   to [?him] they are stran[ge]rs & while short Prefaces are often turned over [without] an hearing as the most uninteresting part of a book long ones can not expect a better fate so I must go on to conclude

To the Public also I return my hearty acknowledgments & however awkardly I may write them here I feel them at heart as sincerely as any one can do   in fact I ought for I have met with a success that I never dare have hoped to realize before I met it.

[lines then deleted] I leave the following poems to speak for themselves – my hopes of success are as warm as ever & I feel that confidence in my readers former kindness to rest satisfied that if the work is worthy the reward it is seeking it will meet it & if not it must share the fate of other broken ambitions & fade away

PREFACE

1827

PREFACES are such customary things, and so often repeated, that I think good ones cannot always be expected; and I am glad that they are so, for it gives me an opportunity of saying something which I am anxious to say, and at the same time leaves me the hope that I shall be pardoned for saying it so ill. I feel desirous to return thanks to my friends, who, I am happy to say, are too numerous to speak of here in any other than a general manner. *[followed immediately in the published version by]*

To the Public, also, I return my hearty acknowledgments; and however awkwardly I may write them here, I feel them at heart as sincerely as any one can do; in fact, I ought, for I have met with a success that I never dare have hoped to realize, before I met it.

I leave the following Poems to speak for themselves, – my hopes of success are as warm as ever, and I feel that confidence in my readers' former kindness, to rest satisfied, that if the work is worthy the reward it is seeking, it will meet it; if not, it must share the fate of other broken ambitions, and fade away. I hope

I hope my low station in life will not be set off as a foil against my verses & I am sure I do not wish to bring it forward as an excuse for any imperfections that may be found in them *[lines deleted]* I cannot conclude without making an apology for the long delay in publishing these Poems which I am sure I will be readily forgiven when it is known that severe illness was the cause. I have said this last which in other respects ought to have been shown first. But I did it purposly because I felt assured that my readers would not consider their dissapointments (if they were dissapointed) as matters of precedence when they knew the cause but on the contrary might think that an apology in such a case was not nessesary even at the conclusion.

[after 5 September1826]

my low station in life will not be set off as a foil against my verses, and I am sure I do not wish to bring it forward as an excuse for any imperfections that may be found in them. I cannot conclude without making an apology for the long delay in publishing these Poems, which, I am sure will be readily forgiven when it is known that severe illness was the cause.

JANUARY

January
A Winters Day

[autumn 1823 –June 1825]

Dithering[1] & keen the winter comes
While comfort flyes to close shut rooms
& sees the snow in feathers pass
Winnowing by the window glass
& unfelt tempests howl & beat   5
Above his head in corner seat
& musing oer the changing scene
Farmers behind the tavern screne
Sit – or wi elbow idly prest
On hob reclines the corners guest   10
Reading the news to mark again
The bankrupt lists or price of grain
Or old mores anual prophecys
That many a theme for talk supplys
Whose almanacks thumbd pages swarm   15
Wi frost & snow & many a storm
& wisdom gossipd from the stars
Of politics & bloody wars
He shakes his head & still proceeds
Neer doubting once of what he reads   20
All wonders are wi faith supplyd
Bible at once & weather guide
Puffing the while his red tipt pipe
Dreaming oer troubles nearly ripe
Yet not quite lost in profits way   25
He ll turn to next years harvest day
& winters leisure to regale
Hopes better times & sips his ale
While labour still pursues his way
& braves the tempest as he may   30
The t[h]resher first thro darkness deep
Awakes the mornings winter sleep
Scaring the owlet from her prey
Long before she dreams of day
That bli[n]ks above head on the mow   35

JANUARY

1827

WITHERING and keen the Winter comes,
While Comfort flies to close-shut rooms,
And sees the snow in feathers pass
Winnowing by the window-glass;
Whilst unfelt tempests howl and beat   5
Above his head in chimney-seat.
    Now, musing o'er the changing scene,
Farmers behind the tavern-screen
Collect; – with elbow idly press'd
On hob, reclines the corner's guest,   10
Reading the news, to mark again
The bankrupt lists, or price of grain;
Or old Moore's annual prophecies
Of flooded fields and clouded skies;
Whose Almanac's thumb'd pages swarm   15
With frost and snow, and many a storm,
And wisdom, gossip'd from the stars,
Of politics and bloody wars.
He shakes his head, and still proceeds,
Nor doubts the truth of what he reads: 20
All wonders are with faith supplied, –
Bible, at once, or weather-guide.
Puffing the while his red-tipt pipe,
He dreams o'er troubles nearly ripe;
Yet, not quite lost in profit's way,   25
He'll turn to next year's harvest-day,
And, Winter's leisure to regale,
Hope better times, and – sip his ale.

Watching the mice that squeaks below
& foddering boys sojourn again
By ryhme hung hedge & frozen plain
Shuffling thro the sinking snows
Blowing his fingers as he goes   40
To were the stock in bellowings hoarse
Call for their meals in dreary close
& print full many a hungry track
Round circling hedge that guards the stack
Wi higgling tug he cuts the hay   45
& bares the forkfull loads away
& morn & evening daily throws
The little heaps upon the snows
The shepherd too in great coat wrapt
& straw bands round his stockings lapt   50
Wi plodding dog that sheltering steals
To shun the wind behind his heels
Takes rough & smooth the winter weather
& paces thro the snow together
While in the fields the lonly plough   55
Enjoys its frozen sabbath now
& horses too pass time away
In leisures hungry holiday
Rubbing & lunging round the yard
Dreaming no doubt of summer sward   60
As near wi idle pace they draw
To brouze the upheapd cribs of straw
While whining dogs wi hungry roar
Crowd around the kitchen door
Or when their scanty meal is done   65
Creep in the straw the cold to shun
& old hens scratting all the day
Seeks curnels chance may throw away
Pausing to pick the seed & grain
Then dusting up the chaff again   70
While in the barn holes hid from view
The cats their patient watch pursue
For birds which want in flocks will draw
From woods & fields to pick the straw
The soodling boy that saunters round   75

[autumn 1823 – June 1825]

1827

The yard on homward dutys bound
Now fills the troughs for noisy hogs
Oft asking aid from barking dogs
That tuggles at each flopping ear
Of such as scramble on too near   80
Or circld round wi thirsty stock
That for his swinging labours flock
At clanking pump his station takes
Half hid in mist their breathing makes
Or at the pond before the door   85
Which every night leaves frozen oer
Wi heavy beetle splinters round
The glossy ice wi jarring sound
While huddling geese as half asleep
Doth round the imprisond water creep   90
Silent & sad to wait his aid
& soon as ere a hole is made
They din his ears wi pleasures cry
& hiss at all that ventures nigh
Splashing wi jealous joys & vain   95
Their fill ere it be froze again
& woodstack climbs at maids desire
Throwing down faggots for the fire
Were stealing time he often stands
To warm his half froze tingling hands   100
The schoolboy still in dithering joys
Pastime in leisure hours employs
& be the weather as it may
Is never at a loss for play
Rolling up jiant heaps of snow   105
As noontide frets its little thaw
Making rude things of various names
Snow men or aught their fancy frames
Till numbd wi cold they quake away
& join at hotter sports to play   110
Kicking wi many a flying bound
The foot ball oer the frozen ground
Or seeking bright glib ice to play
To sailing slide the hours away
As smooth & quick as shadows run   115

[autumn 1823 – June 1825]

The schoolboy still, with dithering joys,
In pastime leisure hours employs, 30
And, be the weather as it may,
Is never at a loss for play:

Making rude forms of various names,
Snow-men, or aught his fancy frames;
Till, numb'd and shivering, he resorts 35
To brisker games and warmer sports –
Kicking, with many a flying bound,
The football o'er the frozen ground;
Or seeking bright glib ice, to play
And slide the wintry hours away, 40
As quick and smooth as shadows run,

1827

When clouds in autumn pass the sun
Some hurrying rambles eager take
To skait upon the meadow lake
Scaring the snipe from her retreat
From shelving banks unfrozen seat   120
Or running brook were icy spars
Which the pale sunlight specks wi stars
Shoots crizzling oer the restless tide
To many a likness petrified
Were fancy often stoops to pore   125
& turns again to wonder more
The more hen too wi fear opprest
Starts from her reedy shelterd rest
Bustling to get from foes away
& scarcly flies more fast then they   130
Skaiting along wi curving springs
Wi arms spread out like herons wings
They race away for pleasures sake
A hunters speed along the lake
& oft neath trees were ice is thin   135
Meet narrow scapes from breaking in
Again the robin waxes tame
& ventures pitys crumbs to claim
Picking the trifles off the snow
Which dames on purpose daily throw   140
& perching on the window sill
Were memory recolecting still
Knows the last winters broken pane
& there he hops & peeps again
The clouds of starnels dailey fly   145
Blackening thro the evening sky
To whittleseas reed wooded mere
& ozier holts by rivers near
& many a mingld swathy crowd
Rook crow & jackdaw noising loud   150
Fly too & fro to dreary fen
Dull winters weary flight agen
Flopping on heavy wings away
As soon as morning wakens grey
& when the sun sets round & red   155

[autumn 1823 – June 1825]

When clouds in autumn pass the sun.
Some, hurrying rambles eager take
To skait upon the meadow lake,
Scaring the snipe from her retreat,   45
From shelving banks in frozen seat;
Or running brook, where icy spars,
Which the pale sun-light specks with stars,
Shoot crizzling o'er the restless tide,
To many a likeness petrified.   50

The moor-hen, too, with fear opprest,
Starts from her reedy shelter'd rest,

As skaiting by, with curving springs,
And arms outspread like heron's wings,
They race away, for pleasure's sake,   55
With hunter's speed along the lake.

    Blackening through the evening sky,
In clouds the starlings daily fly
To Whittlesea's reed-wooded mere,
And osier holts by rivers near;   60
Whilst many a mingled swarthy crowd, –
Rook, crow, and jackdaw, – noising loud,
Fly to and fro to dreary fen,
Dull Winter's weary flight again;
They flop on heavy wings away   65
As soon as morning wakens grey,
And, when the sun sets round and red,

1827

Returns to naked woods to bed
Wood pigeons too in flocks appear
By hunger tamd from timid fear
They mid the sheep unstartld steal
& share wi them a scanty meal 160
Picking the green leaves want bestows
Of turnips sprouting thro the snows
The sun soon creepeth out of sight
Behind the woods – & running night
Makes haste to shut the days dull eye 165
& grizzles oer the chilly sky
Dark deep & thick by day forsook
As cottage chimneys sooty nook
While maidens fresh as summer roses
Joining from the distant closes 170
Haste home wi yokes & swinging pail
& thresher too sets by his flail
& leaves the mice at peace agen
To fill their holes wi stolen grain
& owlets glad his toils are oer 175
Swops by him as he shuts the door
The shepherd seeks his cottage warm
& tucks his hook beneath his arm
& weary in the cold to roam
Scenting the track that leadeth home 180
His dog wi swifter pace proceeds
& barks to urge his masters speed
Then turns & looks him in the face
& trotts before wi mending pace
Till out of whistle from the swain 185
He sits him down & barks again
Anxious to greet the opend door
& meet the cottage fire once more
The robin that wi nimble eye
Glegs round a danger to espy 190
Now pops from out the opend door
From crumbs half left upon the floor
Nor wipes his bill on perching chair
Nor stays to clean a feather there
Scard at the cat that sliveth in 195

[autumn 1823 – June 1825]

Return to naked woods to bed.

    The sun is creeping out of sight
Behind the woods – whilst running Night   70
Hastens to shut the Day's dull eye,
And grizzle o'er the chilly sky.

Now maidens, fresh as summer roses,
Journeying from the distant closes,
Haste home with yokes and swinging pail: 75
The thresher, too, sets by his flail,
And leaves the mice at peace again
To fill their holes with stolen grain;
Whilst owlets, glad his toils are o'er,
Swoop by him as he shuts the door.   80
    Bearing his hook beneath his arm,
The shepherd seeks the cottage warm;
And, weary in the cold to roam,
Scenting the track that leads him home,
His dog goes swifter o'er the mead,   85
Barking to urge his master's speed;
Then turns, and looks him in the face,
And trots before with mending pace,
Till, out of whistle from the swain,
He sits him down and barks again,   90
Anxious to greet the open'd door,
And meet the cottage-fire once more.

*[immediately followed, in a new verse paragraph, by 'The shutter
closed, the lamp alight', below]* [2]

A chance from evenings glooms to win
To jump on chairs or tables nigh
Seeking what plunder may supply
The childerns litterd scraps to thieve
Or aught that negligence may leave   200
Creeping when huswives cease to watch
Or dairey doors are off the latch
On cheese or butter to regale
Or new milk reeking in the pale
The hedger now in leather coat   205
From wood land wilds & fields remote
After a journey far & slow
Knocks from his shoes the caking snow
& opes the welcome creaking door
Throwing his faggot on the floor   210
& at his listning wifes desire
To eke afresh the blazing fire
Wi sharp bill cuts the hazel bands
Then sits him down to warm his hands
& tell in labours happy way   215
His story of the passing day
While as the warm blaze cracks & gleams
The supper reeks in savoury steams
Or keetle simmers merrily
& tinkling cups are set for tea   220
Thus doth the winters dreary day
From morn to evening wear away

[autumn 1823 – June 1825]

A Cottage Evening[3]

[autumn 1823 – June 1825]

The shutte[r]s closd the lamp alight
The faggot chopt & blazing bright
The shepherd from his labour free
Dancing his childern on his knee
Or toasting sloe boughs sputtering ripe   5
Or smoaking glad his puthering pipe
While underneath his masters seat
The tird dog lies in slumbers sweet
Startling & whimpering in his sleep
Chasing still the straying sheep   10
The cat rolld round in vacant chair
Or leaping childerns knees to lair
Or purring on the warmer hearth
Sweet chorus to the crickets mirth
The red cap hanging over head   15
In cage of wire is perchd abed
Slumbering in his painted feathers
Unconcous of the outdoor weathers
& things wi out the cottage walls
Meet comfort as the evening falls   20
As happy in the winters dearth
As those around the blazing hearth
The ass frost drove from off the moors
Were storms thro naked bushes roars
& not a leaf or sprig of green   25
On ground or quaking bush is seen
Save grey veind ivys hardy pride
Round old trees by the common side
Litterd wi straw now dozes warm
Neath the yard hovel from the storm   30
The swine well fed & in the sty
& fowl snug perchd in hovel nigh
Wi head in feathers safe asleep
Were fox find neer a hole to creep
& geese that gabble in their dreams   35

1827

The shutter closed, the lamp alight,
The faggot chopt and blazing bright –
The shepherd now, from labour free, 95
Dances his children on his knee;

While, underneath his master's seat,
The tired dog lies in slumbers sweet,
Starting and whimpering in his sleep,
Chasing still the straying sheep. 100
The cat's roll'd round in vacant chair,
Or leaping children's knees to lair –
Or purring on the warmer hearth,
Sweet chorus to the cricket's mirth. –
The redcap, hanging over head, 105
In cage of wire is perch'd a-bed;
Slumbering in his painted feathers,
Unconscious of the out-door weathers:
Ev'n things without the cottage walls
Meet comfort as the evening falls, – 110
As happy in the Winter's dearth
As those around the blazing hearth. –
The ass, (frost-driven from the moor,
Where storms through naked bushes roar,
And not a leaf or sprig of green, 115
On ground or quaking bush, is seen,
Save grey-vein'd ivy's hardy pride,
Round old trees by the common side)
Litter'd with straw, now dozes warm,
Beneath his shed, from snow and storm: 120
The swine are fed and in the stye;
And fowls snug perch'd in hovel nigh,
With head in feathers safe asleep,
Where foxes cannot hope to creep;
And geese are gabbling in their dreams 125

Of litterd corn & thawing streams
The sparrow too their daily guest
Is in the cottage eves at rest
& robin small & smaller wren
Are in their warm holes safe agen   40
From falling snows that winnow bye
The hovels were they nightly lye
& ague winds that shake the tree
Were other birds are forcd to be
The huswife busy night & day   45
Cleareth the supper things away
While jumping cat starts from her seat
& streaking up on weary feet
The dog wakes at the welcome tones
That calls him up to pick the bones   50
On corner walls a glittering row
Hang fire irons less for use then show
Tongues bright wi huswifes rubbing toil
Who d sooner burn her hands then soil
When sticks want mending up & when   55
Mores sought to eke the blaze agen
& sifter dangling by their side
& poker in the fire untryd
& horshoe brightend as a spell
Witchcrafts evil powers to quell   60
& warming pan reflecting bright
The crackling blazes twittering light
That hangs the corner wall to grace
& seldom taken from its place
Save when the winter keener falls   65
Searching thro the cottage walls
Then quaking from the cottage fire
Warm beds as comforts they require
Yet still tis bright as gold can be
& childern often peep to see   70
Their laughing faces as they pass
Gleam on the lid as plain as glass
Things cleard away then down she sits
& tells her tales by starts & fits
Not willing to loose time or toil   75

[autumn 1823 – June 1825]

Of litter'd corn and thawing streams. –
The sparrow, too, a daily guest,
Is in the cottage eaves at rest:
And robin small, and smaller wren,
Are in their warm holes safe again   130
From falling snows, that winnow by
The hovels where they nightly lie,
And ague winds, that shake the tree
Where other birds are forc'd to be. –
    The housewife, busy night and day,   135
Clears the supper-things away;
The jumping cat starts from her seat;
And stretching up on weary feet
The dog wakes at the welcome tones
That call him up to pick the bones.   140
    On corner walls, a glittering row,
Hang fire-irons – less for use than show;

With horse-shoe brighten'd, as a spell,
Witchcraft's evil powers to quell;
And warming-pan, reflecting bright   145
The crackling blazes' flickering light,
That hangs the corner wall to grace,
Nor oft is taken from its place:

There in its mirror, bright as gold,
The children peep, and straight behold   150
Their laughing faces, whilst they pass,
Gleam on the lid as plain as glass. –
    Supper removed, the mother sits,
And tells her tales by starts and fits.
Not willing to lose time or toil,   155

1827

She knits or sues & talks the while
Somthing as may be warnings found
To the young listners gaping round
Of boys who in her early day
Strolld to the meadow lake to play   80
& skaited races void of fear
Oer deeps or shallows any were
Till willows oer the brink inclind
Shelterd the water from the wind
& left it scarcly crizzld oer   85
When one plopt in to rise no more
& how upon a market night
When near a star bestowed its light
A farmers shepherd oer his glass
Forgot that he had woods to pass   90
Who overtook by darkness deep
Had been to sell his masters sheep
Till coming wi his startld horse
To were two roads a hollow cross
Were lone guide when a stranger strays   95
A white post points four different ways
There by the woodsides lonly gate
A murdering robber lay in wait
The frighted horse wi broken rein
Stood at the stable door again   100
But none came home to fill his rack
Or take the saddle from his back
The saddle it was all he bore
The man was seen alive no more
In her young days beside the wood   105
The gibbet in its terror stood
Tho now all gone tis not forgot
Still dreaded as a haunted spot
& from her memory oft repeats
Witches dread powers & fairey feats   110
How one has oft been known to prance
In cowcribs like a coach to france
& rid on sheep trays from the fold
A race horse speed to burton hold
To join the midnight mysterys rout   115

[autumn 1823 – June 1825]

She knits or sews, and talks the while
Something, that may be warnings found
To the young listeners gaping round –
Of boys who in her early day
Stroll'd to the meadow-lake to play, 160

Where willows, o'er the bank inclined,
Shelter'd the water from the wind,
And left it scarcely crizzled o'er –
When one sank in, to rise no more!
And how, upon a market-night, 165
When not a star bestow'd its light,
A farmer's shepherd, o'er his glass,
Forgot that he had woods to pass:
And having sold his master's sheep,
Was overta'en by darkness deep. 170
How, coming with his startled horse,
To where two roads a hollow cross;
Where, lone guide when a stranger strays,
A white post points four different ways,
Beside the woodride's lonely gate 175
A murdering robber lay in wait.
The frighten'd horse, with broken rein
Stood at the stable-door again;
But none came home to fill his rack,
Or take the saddle from his back: 180
The saddle – it was all he bore –
The man was seen alive no more! –
In her young days, beside the wood,
The gibbet in its terror stood:
Though now decay'd, 'tis not forgot, 185
But dreaded as a haunted spot. –
    She from her memory oft repeats
Witches' dread powers and fairy feats:
How one has oft been known to prance
In cowcribs, like a coach, to France, 190
And ride on sheep-trays from the fold
A race-horse speed to Burton-hold;
To join the midnight mystery's rout,

1827

Were witches meet the year about
& how when met wi unawares
They instant turn to cats or hares
& race along wi hellish flight
Now here & there & out of sight   120
& how the tother tiny things
Will leave their moonlight meadow rings
& unpercievd thro keyholes creep
When alls in bed & fast asleep
& crowd in cupboards as they please   125
As thick as mites in rotten cheese
To feast on what the cotter leaves
For mice ant reckond bigger thieves
They take away too well as eat
& still the huswifes eye they cheat   130
Nothing to miss as other thieves
Alls left the same as she percieves
In spite of all the crowds that swarm
In cottage small & larger farm
That thro each key hole pop & pop   135
Like wasps into a grocers shop
Wi all the things that they can win
From chance to put their plunders in
The shells of wallnuts split in two
By crows who wi the curnels flew   140
& acorn cups by stock doves pluckt
& eggshells by a cuckoo suckt
That hold what ever things they please
Stole tea or sugar bread or cheese
Wi broad leaves of the sycamore   145
To rap as cloths their daintys oer
& hazel nutts when they regale
In cellars brought to hold their ale
Wi bungholes squirrels bored well
To get the curnel from the shell   150
Or maggots a way out to win
When all was eat that grew within
& be the key holes ere so high
Rush poles a laders help supply
Were soft the climbers fearless treads[4]   155

[autumn 1823 – June 1825]

Where witches meet the yews about:
And how, when met with unawares, 195
They turn at once to cats or hares,
And race along with hellish flight,
Now here, now there, now out of sight! –
And how the other tiny things
Will leave their moonlight meadow-rings, 200
And, unperceiv'd, through key-holes creep,
When all around have sunk to sleep,

To feast on what the cotter leaves, –
Mice are not reckon'd greater thieves.
They take away, as well as eat, 205
And still the housewife's eye they cheat,

In spite of all the folks that swarm
In cottage small and larger farm;
They through each key-hole pop and pop,
Like wasps into a grocer's shop, 210
With all the things that they can win
From chance to put their plunder in; –
As shells of walnuts, split in two
By crows, who with the kernels flew;
Or acorn-cups, by stock-doves pluck'd, 215
Or egg-shells by a cuckoo suck'd;

With broad leaves of the sycamore
They clothe their stolen dainties o'er:
And when in cellar they regale,
Bring hazel-nuts to hold their ale; 220
With bung-holes bor'd by squirrels well,
To get the kernel from the shell;
Or maggots a way out to win,
When all is gone that grew within:
And be the key-holes e'er so high, 225
Rush poles a ladder's help supply,
Where soft the climbers fearless tread,

On spindles made of benty threads
& foul or fair or dark the night
Their wild fire lamps are ready light
For which full many a daring crime
Is acted in the summer time   160
When glowworms found in lanes remote
Is murderd for its shining coat
& put in flowers that nature weaves
Wi hollow shapes & silken leaves
Such as the canterbury bell   165
Serving for lamp or lanthorn well
Or following wi unwearied watch
The flight of one they cannot match
As silence sliveth upon sleep[5]
Or thieves by dozing watchdogs creep   170
They steal from Jack a lanthorns tails
A light whose guidance never fails
To aid them in the darkest night
& guide their plundering steps aright
Rattling away in printless tracks   175
Some horsd on beetles glossy backs
Go wisking on & others hie
As fast as loaded moths can flye
Some urge the morning cock to shun
The hardest gallop mice can run   180
In chariots lolling at their ease
Made of what ere their fancys please
Things that in childhoods memory dwells
Scoopd crow-pot-stones or cockle shells
Wi weels at hand of mallow seeds   185
Were childish sports were stringing beads
& thus equipd they softly pass
Like shadows on the summer grass
& drive away in troops together
Just as the spring wind drives a feather   190
They ride oer insects as a stone
Nor bruize a limb nor brake a bone
As light as happy dreams they creep
Nor brake the feeblest link of sleep
A midgeon in their road abed   195

[autumn 1823 – June 1825]

On spindles made of spiders' thread.
And foul, or fair, or dark the night,
Their wild-fire lamps are burning bright: 230
For which full many a daring crime
Is acted in the summer time; –
When glow-worm found in lanes remote
Is murder'd for its shining coat,
And put in flowers, that Nature weaves   235
With hollow shapes and silken leaves,
Such as the Canterbury bell,
Serving for lamp or lantern well;
Or, following with unwearied watch
The flight of one they cannot match,   240
As silence sliveth upon sleep,
Or thieves by dozing watch-dogs creep,
They steal from Jack-a-Lantern's tails
A light, whose guidance never fails
To aid them in the darkest night   245
And guide their plundering steps aright.
Rattling away in printless tracks,
Some, housed on beetles' glossy backs,
Go whisking on – and others hie
As fast as loaded moths can fly: 250
Some urge, the morning cock to shun,
The hardest gallop mice can run,
In chariots, lolling at their ease,
Made of whate'er their fancies please; –
Things that in childhood's memory dwell –   255
Scoop'd crow-pot-stone, or cockle-shell,
With wheels at hand of mallow seeds,
Where childish sport was stringing beads;
And thus equipp'd, they softly pass
Like shadows on the summer-grass,   260
And glide away in troops together
Just as the Spring-wind drives a feather.

As light as happy dreams they creep,
Nor break the feeblest link of sleep:
A midge, if in their road a-bed,   265

Neer feels the wheels run oer his head
But sleeps till sunrise calls him up
Unconscous of the passing troop
Thus dames the winter night regales
Wi wonders never ceasing tales   200
While in the corner ill at ease
Or crushing tween their fathers knees
The childern silent all the while
& een repressd the laugh or smile
Quak[e] wi the ague chills of fear   205
& tremble while they love to hear
Startling while they the tales recall
At their own shadows on the wall
Till the old clock that strikes unseen
Behind the picture pasted screene   210
Were Eve & Adam still agree
To rob lifes fatal apple tree
Counts over bed times hour of rest
& bids each be sleep[s] fearful guest
She then her half told tales will leave   215
To finish on tomorrows eve
The childern cringe away to bed
& up the ladder softly tread
Scarce daring from their fearful joys
To look behind or make a noise   220
Nor speak a word but still as sleep
They secret to their pillows creep
& whisper oer in terrors way
The prayers they dare no louder say
& hide their heads behind the cloaths   225
& try in vain to seek repose
While yet to fancys sleepless eye
Witches on sheep trays gallop bye
& faireys like to rising sparks
Swarm twittering round them in the dark   230
Till sleeps⁵ creeps nigh to ease their cares
& drops upon them unawares
O spirit of the days gone bye⁶
Sweet childhoods fearful extacy
The witching spells of winter nights   235

[autumn 1823 – June 1825]

Feels not the wheels run o'er his head,
But sleeps till sunrise calls him up,
Unconscious of the passing troop. –
    Thus dame the winter-night regales
With wonder's never-ceasing tales;   270
While in a corner, ill at ease,
Or crushing 'tween their father's knees,
The children – silent all the while –
And e'en repressed the laugh or smile –
Quake with the ague chills of fear,   275
And tremble though they love to hear;
Starting, while they the tales recall,
At their own shadows on the wall:
Till the old clock, that strikes unseen
Behind the picture-pasted screen   280
Where Eve and Adam still agree
To rob Life's fatal apple-tree,
Counts over bed-time's hour of rest,
And bids each be Sleep's fearful guest.
She then her half-told tales will leave   285
To finish on to-morrow's eve. –
The children steal away to-bed,
And up the ladder softly tread;
Scarce daring – from their fearful joys –
To look behind or make a noise;   290
Nor speak a word! but still as sleep
They secret to their pillows creep,
And whisper o'er, in terror's way,
The prayers they dare no louder say;
Then hide their heads behind the clothes,   295
And try in vain to seek repose:
While yet, to fancy's sleepless eye,
Witches on sheep-trays gallop by,
And fairies, like a rising spark,
Swarm twittering round them in the dark;   300
Till sleep creeps nigh to ease their cares,
And drops upon them unawares.
    Oh! spirit of the days gone by –
Sweet childhood's fearful ecstasy!
The witching spells of winter nights,   305

1827

Were are they fled wi their delights
When listning on the corner seat
The winter evenings length to cheat
I heard my mothers memory tell
Tales super[s]tition loves so well 240
Things said or sung a thousand times
In simple prose or simpler ryhmes
Ah were is page of poesy
So sweet as theirs was wont to be
The majic wonders that decievd 245
When fictions were as truths believd
The fairey feats that once prevaild
Told to delight & never faild
Were are they now their fears & sighs
& tears from founts of happy eyes 250
Breathless suspense & all their crew
To what wild dwelling have they flew
I read in books but find them not
For poesy hath its youth forgot
I hear them told to childern still 255
But fear near numbs my spirits chill
I still see faces pale wi dread
While mine coud laugh at what is said
See tears imagind woes supply
While mine wi real cares are dry 260
Were are they gone the joys & fears
The links the life of other years
I thought they bound around my heart
So close that we coud never part
But reason like a winters day 265
Nipt childhoods visions all away
Nor left behind one withering flower
To cherish in a lonly hour
Memory may yet the themes repeat
But childhoods heart doth cease to beat 270
At storys reasons sterner lore
Turneth like gossips from her door
The majic fountain were the head
Rose up just as the startld maid
Was stooping from the weedy brink 275

[autumn 1823 – June 1825]

Where are they fled with their delights?
When list'ning on the corner seat,
The winter evening's length to cheat,
I heard my mother's memory tell
Tales Superstition loves so well: –   310
Things said or sung a thousand times,
In simple prose or simpler rhymes!
Ah! where is page of poesy
So sweet as this was wont to be?
The magic wonders that deceived,   315
When fictions were as truths believed;
The fairy feats that once prevail'd,
Told to delight, and never fail'd:
Where are they now, their fears and sighs,
And tears from founts of happy eyes?   320

I read in books, but find them not,
For Poesy hath its youth forgot:
I hear them told to children still,
But fear numbs not my spirits chill:
I still see faces pale with dread,   325
While mine could laugh at what is said;
See tears imagined woes supply,
While mine with real cares are dry.
Where are they gone? – the joys and fears,
The links, the life of other years?   330
I thought they twined around my heart
So close, that we could never part;
But Reason, like a winter's day,
Nipp'd childhood's visions all away,
Nor left behind one withering flower   335
To cherish in a lonely hour.
Memory may yet the themes repeat,
But Childhood's heart hath ceased to beat
At tales, which Reason's sterner lore
Turns like weak gossips from her door: 340
The Magic Fountain, where the head
Rose up, just as the startled maid
Was stooping from the weedy brink

1827

To dip her pitcher in to drink
That did its half hid mystery tell
To smooth its hair & use it well
Who doing as it bade her do
Turnd to a king & lover too   280
The tale of Cinderella told
The winter thro & never old
The faireys favourite & friend
Who made her happy in the end
The pumpkin that at her approach   285
Was turnd into a golden coach
The rats that faireys majic knew
& instantly to horses grew
& coachmen ready at her call
To drive her to the princes ball   290
With fur changd jackets silver lind
& tails hung neath their hats behind
Were soon as met the princes sight
She made his heart ach all the night
The golden glove wi fingers small   295
She lost while dancing in the hall
That was on every finger tryd
& fitted hers & none beside
When cinderella soon as seen
Was woo d & won & made a queen   300
The boy that did the jiants slay
& gave his mothers cows away
For majic mask that day or night
When on woud keep him out of sight
& running beans not such as weaves   305
Round poles the hight of cottage eves
But majic ones that travelld high
Some steeples journeys up the sky
& reachd a jiants dwelling there
A cloud built castle in the air   310
Were venturing up the fearfull height
That servd him climbing half the night
He searchd the jiants coffers oer
& never wanted wealth no more
While like a lion scenting food   315

[autumn 1823 – June 1825]

To dip her pitcher in to drink,
That did its half-hid mystery tell   345
To smooth its hair, and use it well;
Which, doing as it bade her do,
Turn'd to a king and lover too.
The tale of Cinderella, told
The winter through, and never old: 350

The pumpkin that, at her approach,
Was turn'd into a golden coach;
The rats that fairies' magic knew,
And instantly to horses grew;
The coachmen ready at her call,   355
To drive her to the Prince's ball,
With fur-changed jackets silver lined,
And tails hung 'neath their hats behind;

The golden glove, with fingers small,
She lost while dancing in the hall,   360
That was on every finger tried,
And fitted hers, and none beside,
When Cinderella, soon as seen,
Was woo'd and won, and made a Queen.
The Boy that did the Giant slay,   365
And gave his mother's cows away
For magic mask, that day or night,
When on, would keep him out of sight.
The running bean, – not such as weaves
Round poles the height of cottage eaves,   370
But magic one, – that travell'd high
Some steeple's journey up the sky,
And reach'd a giant's dwelling there,
A cloud-built castle in the air:
Where, venturing up the fearful height,   375
That served him climbing half the night,
He search'd the giant's coffers o'er,
And never wanted riches more;
While, like a lion scenting food,

1827

The jiant roard in hungry mood
A storm of threats that might suffice
To frieze the hottest blood to ice
& make when heard however bold
The strongest heart strings cramp wi cold   320
But mine sleeps on thro fear & dread
& terrors that might wake the dead
When like a lion in the wood
He snufts & tracks the scent of blood
& vows if aught falls in his power   325
He ll grind their very bones to flower
I hear it now nor dream of harm
The storm is settld to a calm
Those fears are dead   what will not dye
In fading lifes mortality   330
Those truths are fled & left behind
A real world & doubting mind

[autumn 1823 – June 1825]

The giant roar'd, in hungry mood,   380
A storm of threats that might suffice
To freeze the hottest blood to ice.

    I hear it now, nor dream of woes;
The storm is settled to repose.
Those fears are dead! – What will not die   385
In fading Life's mortality?
Those truths have fled, and left behind
A real world and doubting mind.

1827

FEBRUARY

FEBRUARY – A THAW[7]

[autumn 1823 – June 1825]

The snow is gone from cottage tops
The thatch moss glows in brighter green
& eves in quick succession drops
Were grinning icicles hath been
Pit patting wi a pleasant noise   5
In tubs set by the cottage door
& ducks & geese wi happy joys
Douse in the yard pond brimming oer

The sun peeps thro the window pane
Which childern mark wi laughing eye   10
& in the wet street steal again
To tell each other spring is nigh
& as young hope the past recalls
In playing groups will often draw
Building beside the sunny walls   15
Their spring-play-huts of sticks or straw

& oft in pleasures dreams they hie
Round homsteads by the village side
Scratting the hedgrow mosses bye
Were painted pooty shells abide   20
Mistaking oft the ivy spray
For leaves that come wi budding spring
& wondering in their search for play
Why birds delay to build & sing

The milkmaid singing leaves her bed   25
As glad as happy thoughts can be
While magpies chatter oer her head
As jocund in the change as she

February

1827

I

THE snow has left the cottage top;
   The thatch-moss grows in brighter green;
And eaves in quick succession drop,
   Where grinning icicles have been;
Pit-patting with a pleasant noise   5
   In tubs set by the cottage-door;
While ducks and geese, with happy joys,
   Plunge in the yard-pond brimming o'er.

II

The sun peeps through the window-pane;
   Which children mark with laughing eye,   10
And in the wet street steal again,
   To tell each other Spring is nigh:
Then, as young hope the past recalls,
   In playing groups they often draw,
To build beside the sunny walls   15
   Their spring-time huts of sticks or straw.

III

And oft in pleasure's dreams they hie
   Round homesteads by the village side,
Scratching the hedgerow mosses by,
   Where painted pooty shells abide,   20
Mistaking oft the ivy spray
   For leaves that come with budding Spring,
And wond'ring, in their search for play,
   Why birds delay to build and sing.

IV

The milkmaid singing leaves her bed,
   As glad as happy thoughts can be,
While magpies chatter o'er her head
   As jocund in the change as she:

Her cows around the closes stray
Nor lingering wait the foddering boy   30
Tossing the mollhills in their play
& staring round in frolic joy

Ploughmen go whistling to their toils
& yoke again the rested plough
& mingling oer the mellow soils   35
Boys shouts & whips are noising now
The shepherd now is often seen
By warm banks oer his hook to bend
Or oer a gate or stile to lean
Chattering to a passing friend   40

Odd hive bees fancying winter oer
& dreaming in their combs of spring
Creeps on the slab beside their door
& strokes its legs upon its wing
While wild ones half asleep are humming   45
Round snowdrop bells a feeble note
& pigions coo of summer coming
Picking their feathers on the cote

The barking dogs by lane & wood
Drive sheep afield from foddering ground   50
& eccho in her summer mood
Briskly mocks the cheery sound
The flocks as from a prison broke
Shake their wet fle[e]ces in the sun
While following fast a misty smoke   55
Reeks from the moist grass as they run

Nor more behind his masters heels
The dog creeps oer his winter pace
But cocks his tail & oer the fields
Runs many a wild & random chase   60

[autumn 1823 – June 1825]

Her cows around the closes stray,
    Nor ling'ring wait the foddering-boy;   30
Tossing the mole-hills in their play,
    And staring round with frolic joy.

V

The shepherd now is often seen
    Near warm banks o'er his hook to bend;
Or o'er a gate or stile to lean,   35
    Chattering to a passing friend:
Ploughmen go whistling to their toils,
    And yoke again the rested plough;
And, mingling o'er the mellow soils,
    Boys shout, and whips are noising now.   40

VI

The barking dogs, by lane and wood,
    Drive sheep a-field from foddering ground;
And Echo, in her summer mood,
    Briskly mocks the cheering sound.
The flocks, as from a prison broke,   45
    Shake their wet fleeces in the sun,
While, following fast, a misty smoke
    Reeks from the moist grass as they run.

VII

No more behind his master's heels
    The dog creeps on his winter-pace;   50
But cocks his tail, and o'er the fields
    Runs many a wild and random chase,

1827

Following in spite of chiding calls
The startld cat in harmless glee
Scaring her up the weed green walls
Or mossy mottld apple tree

As crows from morning perches flye   65
He barks & follows them in vain
Een larks will catch his nimble eye
& off he starts & barks again
Wi breathless haste & blinded guess
Oft following were the hare hath gone   70
Forgetting in his joys excess
His frolic puppy days are done

The gossips saunter in the sun
As at the spring from door to door
Of matters in the village done   75
& secret newsings mutterd oer
Young girls when they each other meet
Will stand their tales of love to tell
While going on errands down the street
Or fetching water from the well   80

A calm of pleasure listens round
& almost whispers winter bye
While fancy dreams of summer sounds
& quiet rapture fills the eye
The sun beams on the hedges lye   85
The south wind murmurs summer soft
& maids hang out white cloaths to dry
Around the eldern skirted croft

Each barns green thatch reeks in the sun
Its mate the happy sparrow calls   90
& as nest building spring begun
Peeps in the holes about the walls

[autumn 1823 – June 1825]

Following, in spite of chiding calls,
    The startled cat with harmless glee,
Scaring her up the weed-green walls,   55
    Or mossy mottled apple tree.

VIII

As crows from morning perches fly,
    He barks and follows them in vain;
E'en larks will catch his nimble eye,
    And off he starts and barks again,   60
With breathless haste and blinded guess,
    Oft following where the hare hath gone;
Forgetting, in his joy's excess,
    His frolic puppy-days are done!

IX

The hedgehog, from his hollow root,   65
    Sees the wood-moss clear of snow,
And hunts the hedge for fallen fruit –
    Crab, hip, and winter-bitten sloe;

1827

The wren a sunny side the stack
Wi short tail ever on the strunt
Cockd gadding up above his back   95
Again for dancing gnats will hunt

The gladdend swine bolt from the sty
& round the yard in freedom run
Or stretching in their slumbers lye
Beside the cottage in the sun   100
The young horse whinneys to its mate
& sickens from the threshers door
Rubbing the straw yards banded gate
Longing for freedom on the moor

Hens leave their roosts wi cackling calls   105
To see the barn door free from snow
& cocks flye up the mossy walls
To clap their spangld wings & crow
About the steeples sunny top
The jackdaw flocks resemble spring   110
& in the stone archd windows pop
Wi summer noise & wanton wing

The small birds think their wants are oer
To see the snow hills fret again
& from the barns chaff litterd door   115
Betake them to the greening plain
The woodmans robin startles coy
Nor longer at his elbow comes
To peck wi hungers eager joy
Mong mossy stulps the litterd crumbs   120

Neath hedge & walls that screen the wind
The gnats for play will flock together
& een poor flyes odd hopes will find
To venture in the mocking weather

[autumn 1823 – June 1825]

But often check'd by sudden fears,
    As shepherd-dog his haunt espies,   70
He rolls up in a ball of spears,
    And all his barking rage defies.

X

The gladden'd swine bolt from the sty,
    And round the yard in freedom run,
Or stretching in their slumbers lie   75
    Beside the cottage in the sun.
The young horse whinneys to his mate,
    And, sickening from the thresher's door,
Rubs at the straw-yard's banded gate,
    Longing for freedom on the moor.   80

XI

The small birds think their wants are o'er,
    To see the snow-hills fret again,
And, from the barn's chaff-litter'd door,
    Betake them to the greening plain.
The woodman's robin startles coy,   85
    Nor longer to his elbow comes,
To peck, with hunger's eager joy,
    'Mong mossy stulps the litter'd crumbs.

XII

'Neath hedge and walls that screen the wind,
    The gnats for play will flock together;   90
And e'en poor flies some hope will find
    To venture in the mocking weather;

1827

From out their hidy holes again   125
Wi feeble pace they often creep
Along the sun warmd window pane
Like dreaming things that walk in sleep

The mavis thrush wi wild delight
Upon the orchards dripping tree   130
Mutters to see the day so bright
Spring scraps of young hopes poesy
& oft dame stops her burring wheel
To hear the robins note once more
That tutles while he pecks his meal   135
From sweet-briar hips beside the door

The hedghog from its hollow root
Sees the wood moss clear of snow
& hunts each hedge for fallen fruit
Crab hip & winter bitten sloe   140
& oft when checkd by sudden fears
As shepherd dog his haunt espies
He rolls up in a ball of spears
& all his barking rage defies

Thus nature of the spring will dream   145
While south winds thaw but soon again
Frost breaths upon the stiffening stream
& numbs it into ice – the plain
Soon wears its mourning garb of white[8]
& icicles that fret at noon   150
Will eke their icy tails at night
Beneath the chilly stars & moon

Nature soon sickens of her joys
& all is sad & dumb again
Save merry shouts of sliding boys   155
About the frozen furrowd plain

[autumn 1823 – June 1825]

From out their hiding-holes again,
  With feeble pace, they often creep
Along the sun-warm'd window-pane,   95
  Like dreaming things that walk in sleep.

XIII

The mavis thrush with wild delight,
  Upon the orchard's dripping tree,
Mutters, to see the day so bright,
  Fragments of young Hope's poesy: 100
And oft Dame stops her buzzing wheel
  To hear the robin's note once more,
Who tootles while he pecks his meal
  From sweet-briar hips beside the door.

XIV

The sunbeams on the hedges lie,   105
  The south wind murmurs summer soft;
The maids hang out white clothes to dry
  Around the elder-skirted croft:
A calm of pleasure listens round,
  And almost whispers Winter by;   110
While Fancy dreams of Summer's sound,
  And quiet rapture fills the eye.

XV

Thus Nature of the Spring will dream
  While south winds thaw; but soon again
Frost breathes upon the stiff'ning stream,   115
  And numbs it into ice: the plain
Soon wears its mourning garb of white;
  And icicles, that fret at noon,
Will eke their icy tails at night
  Beneath the chilly stars and moon.   120

XVI

Nature soon sickens of her joys,
  And all is sad and dumb again,
Save merry shouts of sliding boys
  About the frozen furrow'd plain.

1827

The foddering boy forgets his song
& silent goes wi folded arms
& croodling shepherds bend along
Crouching to the whizzing storms   160

[autumn 1823 – June 1825]

The foddering-boy forgets his song, 125
   And silent goes with folded arms;
And croodling shepherds bend along,
   Crouching to the whizzing storms.

1827

MARCH

March

[January/February 1824 – June 1825]

March month of "many weathers" wildly comes
In hail & snow & rain & threatning hums
& floods:– while often at his cottage door
The shepherd stands to hear the distant roar
Loosd from the rushing mills & river locks   5
Wi thundering sound & over powering shocks
& headlong hurry thro the meadow brigs
Brushing the leaning willows fingering twigs
In feathering foam & eddy hurrying chase
Rolling a storm oertaken travellers pace   10
From bank to bank along the meadow leas
Spreading & shining like to little seas
While in the pale sunlight a watery brood
Of swopping white birds flock about the flood
Yet winter seems half weary of its toil   15
& round the ploughman on the elting soil
Will thread a minutes sunshine wild & warm
Thro the raggd places of the swimming storm
& oft the shepherd in his path will spye
The little daisey in the wet grass lye   20
That to the peeping sun enlivens gay
Like Labour smiling on an holiday
& were the stunt bank fronts the southern sky
By lanes or brooks were sunbeams love to lye
A cowslip peep will open faintly coy   25
Soon seen & gatherd by a wandering boy
A tale of spring around the distant haze
Seems muttering pleasures wi the lengthning days
Morn wakens mottld oft wi may day stains
& shower drops hang the grassy sprouting plains   30
& on the naked thorns of brassy hue
Drip glistning like a summer dream of dew
While from the hill side freshning forest drops
As one might walk upon their thickening tops
& buds wi young hopes promise seemly swells   35

MARCH

1827

MARCH, month of "many weathers," wildly comes
In hail, and snow, and rain, and threatening hums,
And floods; – while often at his cottage-door
The shepherd stands, to hear the distant roar
Loosed from the rushing mills and river-locks,   5
With thundering sound and overpowering shocks.

From bank to bank, along the meadow lea,
The river spreads, and shines a little sea;
While, in the pale sunlight, a watery brood
Of swopping white birds flock about the flood.   10
   Yet Winter seems half weary of his toil;
And round the ploughmen, on the elting soil,
Will thread a minute's sunshine wild and warm,
Through the ragg'd places of the swimming storm;
And oft the shepherd in his path will spy   15
The little daisy in the wet grass lie,
That to the peeping sun uncloses gay,
Like Labour smiling on a holiday;
And where the steep bank fronts the southern sky,
By lanes or brooks where sunbeams love to lie,   20
A cowslip-peep will open faintly coy,
Soon seen and gather'd by a wondering boy.
   A tale of Spring around the distant haze
Seems muttering pleasures with the lengthening days;
Morn wakens, mottled oft with May-day stains;   25
And shower-drops hang the grassy sprouting plains,
Or on the naked thorns of brassy hue
Drip glistening, like a summer-dream of dew.

Were woodman that in wild seclusion dwells
Wi chopping toil the coming spring dec[i]eves
Of many dancing shadows flowers & leaves
& in his pathway down the mossy wood
Crushes wi hasty feet full many a bud   40
Of early primrose yet if timely spied
Shelterd some old half rotten stump beside
The sight will cheer his solitery hour
& urge his feet to stride & save the flower
Muffld in baffles leathern coat & gloves   45
The hedger toils oft scaring rustling doves
From out the hedgrows who in hunger browze
The chockolate berrys on the ivy boughs
& flocking field fares speckld like the thrush
Picking the red awe from the sweeing bush   50
That come & go on winters chilly wing
& seem to share no sympethy wi spring
The stooping ditcher in the water stands
Letting the furrowd lakes from off the lands
Or splashing cleans the pasture brooks of mud   55
Were many a wild weed freshens into bud
& sprouting from the bottom purply green
The water cresses neath the wave is seen
Which the old woman gladly drags to land
Wi reaching long rake in her tottering hand   60
The ploughman mawls along the doughy sloughs
& often stop their songs to clean their ploughs
From teazing twitch that in the spongy soil
Clings round the colter terryfying toil
The sower striding oer his dirty way   65
Sinks anckle deep in pudgy sloughs & clay
& oer his heavy hopper stoutly leans
Strewing wi swinging arms the pattering beans
Which soon as aprils milder weather gleams
Will shoot up green between the furroed seams   70
The driving boy glad when his steps can trace
The swelling edding as a resting place
Slings from his clotted shoes the dirt around
& feign woud rest him on the solid ground
& sings when he can meet the parting green   75

[January/February 1824 – June 1825]

The woodman, in his pathway down the wood,
Crushes with hasty feet full many a bud   30
Of early primrose; yet if timely spied,
Shelter'd some old half-rotten stump beside,
The sight will cheer his solitary hour,
And urge his feet to stride and save the flower.

The hedger's toils oft scare the doves, that browze   35
The chocolate berries on the ivy boughs,
Or flocking fieldfares, speckled like the thrush,
Picking the berry from the hawthorn bush,
That come and go on Winter's chilling wing,
And seem to share no sympathy with Spring.   40

The ploughmen now along the doughy sloughs
Will often stop their songs, to clean their ploughs
From teazing twitch, that in the spongy soil
Clings round the coulter, interrupting toil.

The sower o'er his heavy hopper leans,   45
Strewing with swinging arms the pattering beans,
Which, soon as April's milder weather gleams,
Will shoot up green between the furrow'd seams.
The driving boy, glad when his steps can trace
The swelling headland as a resting-place,   50
Flings from his clotted shoes the dirt around,
And fain would rest him on the solid ground.

1827

Of rushy balks that bend the lands between
While close behind em struts the nauntling crow
& daws whose heads seem powderd oer wi snow
To seek the worms – & rooks a noisey guest
That on the wind rockd elms prepares her nest					80
On the fresh furrow often drops to pull
The twitchy roots & gathering sticks & wool
Neath trees whose dead twigs litter to the wind
& gaps were stray sheep left their coats behind
While ground larks on a sweeing clump of rushes					85
Or on the top twigs of the oddling bushes
Chirp their "cree creeing" note that sounds of spring
& sky larks meet the sun wi flittering wing
Soon as the morning opes its brightning eye
Large clouds of sturnels blacken thro the sky					90
From oizer holts about the rushy fen
& reed shaw borders by the river Nen
& wild geese regiments now agen repair
To the wet bosom of broad marshes there
In marching coloms & attention all					95
Listning & following their ring leaders call
The shepherd boy that hastens now & then
From hail & snow beneath his sheltering den
Of flags or file leavd sedges tyd in sheaves
Or stubble shocks oft as his eye percieves					100
Sun threads shrink out wi momentary smiles
Wi fancy thoughts his lonliness beguiles
Thinking the struggling winter hourly bye
As down the edges of the distant sky
The hail storm sweeps – & while he stops to strip					105
The stooping hedgbriar of its lingering hip
He hears the wild geese gabble oer his head
& pleasd wi fancys in his musings bred
He marks the figurd forms in which they flye
& pausing follows wi a wondering eye					110
Likening their curious march in curves or rows
To every letter which his memory knows
While far above the solitary crane
Swings lonly to unfrozen dykes again
Cranking a jarring mellancholy cry					115

[January/February 1824 – June 1825]

Not far behind them struts the nauntly crow,
And daw, whose head seems powder'd o'er with snow,
Seeking the worms: the rook, a noisy guest,   55
That on the wind-rock'd elms prepares her nest,
On the fresh furrow often drops, to pull
The twitching roots, or gather sticks and wool,
From trees whose dead twigs litter to the wind,
And gaps where stray sheep left their coats behind;   60
While ground-larks, on a swinging clump of rushes,
Or on the top twigs of the scatter'd bushes,
Chirp their "cree-creery" note, that sounds of Spring;
And sky-larks meet the sun with fluttering wing.

   The shepherd-boy, that hastens now and then   65
From hail and snow beneath his sheltering den
Of flags, or file-leaved sedges tied in sheaves,
Or stubble shocks, oft as his eye perceives
Sun-threads shrink out in momentary smiles,
With fairy thoughts his loneliness beguiles;   70
Thinking the struggling Winter howling by,
As down the edges of the distant sky
The hail-storm sweeps; – and while he stops to strip
The stooping hedgebriar of its lingering hip,
He hears the wild geese gabble o'er his head;   75
Then, pleased with fancies in his musings bred,
He marks the figured forms in which they fly,
And pausing, follows with a wondering eye,
Likening their curious march, in curves or rows,
To every letter which his memory knows;   80
While, far above, the solitary crane
Swings lonely to unfrozen dykes again,
Cranking a jarring melancholy cry

Thro the wild journey of the cheerless sky
Full oft at early seasons mild & fair
March bids farewell wi garlands in her hair
Of hazzel tassles woodbines hairy sprout
& sloe & wild plumb blossoms peeping out   120
In thick set knotts of flowers preparing gay
For aprils reign a mockery of may
That soon will glisten on the earnest eye
Like snow white cloaths hung in the sun to drye
The old dame often stills her burring wheel   125
When the bright sun will thro the window steal
& gleam upon her face & dancing fall
In diamond shadows on the picturd wall
While the white butterflye as in amaze
Will settle on the glossy glass to gaze   130
& oddling bee oft patting passing bye
As if they care to tell her spring was nigh
& smiling glad to see such things once more
Up she will get & potter to the door
& look upon the trees beneath the eves   135
Sweet briar & ladslove swelling into leaves
& damsin trees thick notting into bloom
& goosberry blossoms on the bushes come
& stooping down oft views her garden beds
To see the spring flowers pricking out their heads   140
& from her apron strings she ll often pull
Her sissars out an early bunch to cull
For flower pots on the window board to stand
Were the old hour glass spins its thread of sand
& maids will often mark wi laughing eye   145
In elder were they hang their cloaths to drye
The sharp eyd robin hop from grain to grain
Singing its little summer notes again
As a sweet pledge of Spring the little lambs
Bleat in the varied weather round their dams   150
Or hugh molehill or roman mound behind
Like spots of snow lye shelterd from the wind
While the old yoes bold wi paternal cares
Looses their fears & every danger dares
Who if the shepherds dog but turns his eye   155

[January/February 1824 – June 1825]

Through the wild journey of the cheerless sky.
   Often, at early seasons, mild and fair   85
March bids farewell, with garlands in her hair
Of hazel tassels, woodbine's bushy sprout,
And sloe and wild-plum blossoms peeping out
In thick-set knots of flowers, preparing gay,
For April's reign, a mockery of May.   90

The old dame then oft stills her humming wheel –
When the bright sun-beams through the windows steal
And gleam upon her face, and dancing fall
In diamond shadows on the pictur'd wall;
While the white butterfly, as in amaze,   95
Will settle on the glossy glass to gaze –

And smiling, glad to see such things once more,
Up she will get and totter to the door,
And look upon the trees beneath the eaves –
Sweetbriar and lad's-love – swelling into leaves;   100

And, stooping down, cull from her garden beds
The early blossoms perking out their heads,

In flower-pots on the window-board to stand,
Where the old hour-glass spins its thread of sand.

1827

& stops behind a moment passing bye
Will stamp draw back & then their threats repeat
Urging defiance wi their stamping feet
& stung wi cares hopes cannot recconsile
They stamp & follow till he leaps a stile   160
Or skulking from their threats betakes to flight
& wi the master lessens out of sight
Clowns mark the threetning rage of march pass bye
& clouds wear thin & ragged in the sky
While wi less sudden & more lasting smiles   165
The growing sun their hopes of spring beguiles
Who often at its end remark wi pride
Days lengthen in their visits a "cocks stride"
Dames clean their candlestiks & set them bye
Glad of the makeshift light that eves supply   170
The boy returning home at night from toil
Down lane & close oer footbrig gate & style
Oft trembles into fear & stands to hark
The waking fox renew his short gruff bark
While badgers eccho their dread evening shrieks   175
& to his thrilling thoughts in terror speaks
& shepherds that wi in their hulks remain
Night after night upon the chilly plain
To watch the dropping lambs that at all hours
Come in the quaking blast like early flowers   180
Demanding all the shepherd[s] care who form
Up walls of straw to make their dwelling warm
& round their necks in wary caution tyes
Long shreds of rags in red or purple dyes
Thats meant in danger as a safty spell   185
Like the old yoe that wears a tinkling bell
The sneaking foxes from his thefts to fright
That often seizes the young lambs at night
These when they in their nightly watchings hear
The badgers shrieks can hardly stifle fear   190
They list the noise from woodlands dark recess
Like helpless shrieking woman in distress
& oft as such fears fancying mistery
Believes the dismal yelling sounds to be
For superstitition hath its thousand tales   195

[January/February 1824 – June 1825]

And while the passing clown remarks, with pride,   105
Days lengthen in their visits a "cock's stride,"
She cleans her candlesticks and sets them by,
Glad of the make-shift light that eves supply!
    The boy, retiring home at night from toil,
Down lane and close, o'er footbrig, gate, and stile,   110
Oft trembles into fear, and stands to hark
The waking fox renew his short gruff bark;

And shepherds – that within their hulks remain
Night after night upon the chilly plain,
To watch the dropping lambs, that at all hours   115
Come in the quaking blast like tender flowers –

When in the nightly watch they chance to hear
The badger's shrieks, can hardly stifle fear;
Likening the cry, from woodland's dark recess,
To that of helpless woman in distress: 120

For Superstition hath a thousand tales

1827

To people all his midnight woods & vales
& the dread spot from whence the dismal noise
Mars the night musings of their dark employs
Owns its sad tale to realize their fear
At which their hearts in boyhood achd to hear   200
A maid at night by treacherous love decoyd
Was in that shrieking wood years past destroyd
She went twas said to meet the waiting swain
& home & friends near saw her face again
Mid brakes & thorns that crowded round the dell   205
& matting weeds that had no tongues to tell
He murderd her alone at dead midnight
While the pale moon threw round her sickly light
& loud shrieks left the thickets slumbers deep
That only scard the little birds from sleep   210
When the pale murdere[r]s terror frowning eye
Told its dread errand that the maid shoud dye
Mid thick black thorns her secret grave was made
& th[e]re wi night the murderd girl was laid
When no one saw the deed but god & he   215
& moonlight sparkling thro the sleeping tree
Around – the red breast might at morning steel
There for the worm to meet his morning meal
In fresh turnd moulds that first beheld the sun
Nor knew the deed that dismal night had done   220
Such is the tale that superstition gives
& in her midnight memory ever lives
That makes the boy run by wi wild affright
& shepherds startle on their rounds at night
Now love teazd maidens from their droning wheels   225
At the red hour of sun set sliving steals
From scolding dames to meet their swains agen
Tho water checks their visits oer the plain
They slive were no one sees some wall behind
Or orchard apple trees that stops the wind   230
To talk about springs pleasures hove[r]ing nigh
& happy rambles when the roads get dry
The insect world now sunbeams higher climb
Oft dream of spring & wake before their time
Blue flies from straw stack crawling scarce alive   235

[January/February 1824 – June 1825]

To people all her midnight woods and vales; –
And the dread spot from whence the dismal noise
Mars the night-musings of their dark employs,
Owns its sad tale to realize their fear –   125
A tale their hearts in boyhood ached to hear.
A maid, at night, by treacherous love decoy'd,
Was in that shrieking wood, years past, destroy'd.
She went, 'twas said, to meet the waiting swain;
But home and friends ne'er saw her face again!   130
'Mid brake and thorns that crowded round the dell,
And matting weeds that had no tongue to tell,
He murder'd her alone at dead midnight,
While the pale moon threw round her sickly light.
Loud screams assail'd the thicket's slumbers deep,   135
But only scared the little birds from sleep;
When the pale murderer's terror-frowning eye
Told its dread errand – that the maid should die. –
'Mid thick black thorns her secret grave was made;
And there the unresisting corpse was laid,   140
When no one saw the deed but God and he,
And moonlight sparkling through the sleeping tree.
The Robin-redbreast might at morning steal
There, for the worm to meet his early meal,
In fresh-turn'd moulds which first beheld the sun –   145
Nor know the deed that dismal night had done.
Such is the tale that Superstition gives;
Which in her midnight memory ever lives;
Which makes the boy run by with wild affright,
And shepherds startle on their rounds at night.   150
   Now love-teazed maidens, from the droning wheel,
At the red hour of sun-set, slily steal
From scolding dames, to meet their swains again;
Though water checks their visits o'er the plain:
They slive where no one sees, some wall behind,   155
Or orchard apple-tree that stops the wind,
To talk about Spring's pleasures hovering nigh,
And happy rambles when the roads get dry.
   The insect-world, now sunbeams higher climb,
Oft dream of Spring, and wake before their time.   160

& bees peep out on slabs before the hive
Stroaking their little legs across their wings
& venturing short flight were the snow drop hings
Its silver bell – & winter aconite
Wi buttercup like flowers that shut at night   240
& green leaf frilling round their cups of gold
Like tender maiden muffld from the cold
They sip & find their honey dreams are vain
& feebly hasten to their hives again
& butter flys by eager hopes undone   245
Glad as a child come out to greet the sun
Lost neath the shadow of a sudden shower
Nor left to see tomorrows april flower

[January/February 1824 – June 1825]

Bees stroke their little legs across their wings,
And venture short flights where the snow-drop hings
Its silver bell, and winter aconite
Its butter-cup-like flowers that shut at night,
With green leaf furling round its cup of gold,   165
Like tender maiden muffled from the cold:
They sip, and find their honey-dreams are vain,
Then feebly hasten to their hives again. –
The butterflies, by eager hopes undone,
Glad as a child come out to greet the sun,   170
Beneath the shadow of a sudden shower
Are lost – nor see to-morrow's April flower.

APRIL

APRIL[9]

[March 1822]

The infant april joins the spring
& views its watery skye
As youngling linnet trys its wing
& fears at first to flye
With timid step she ventures on   5
& hardly dares to smile
The blossoms open one by one
& sunny hours beguile

But finer days approacheth yet
With scenes more sweet to charm   10
& suns arive that rise & set
Bright strangers to a storm
& as the birds with louder song
Each mornings glory cheers
With bolder step she speeds along   15
& looses all her fears

In wanton gambols like a child
She tends her early toils
& seeks the buds along the wild
That blossom while she smiles   20
& laughing on with nought to chide
She races with the hours
Or sports by natures lovley side
& fills her lap with flowers

Tho at her birth north cutting gales
Her beautys oft disguise   25
& hopfull blossoms turning pales[10]
Upon her bosom dies

APRIL

1827

I

Now infant April joins the Spring,
    And views the watery sky,
As youngling linnet tries its wing,
    And fears at first to fly;
With timid step she ventures on,   5
    And hardly dares to smile,
Till blossoms open one by one,
    And sunny hours beguile.

II

But finer days are coming yet,
    With scenes more sweet to charm,   10
And suns arrive that rise and set
    Bright strangers to a storm:
Then, as the birds with louder song
    Each morning's glory cheer,
With bolder step she speeds along,   15
    And loses all her fear.

III

In wanton gambols, like a child,
    She tends her early toils,
And seeks the buds along the wild,
    That blossoms while she smiles;   20
Or, laughing on, with nought to chide,
    She races with the Hours,
Or sports by Nature's lovely side,
    And fills her lap with flowers.

Yet ere she seeks another place
& ends her reign in this   30
She leaves us with as fair a face
As ere gave birth to bliss[11]

& fairey month of waking mirth
From whom our joys ensue
Thou early gladder of the earth   35
Thrice welcom here anew
With thee the bud unfolds to leaves
The grass greens on the lea
& flowers their tender boon recieves
To bloom & smile with thee   40

The shepherds on thy pasture walks
The first fair cows lip finds
Whose tufted flowers on slender stalks
Keep nodding to the winds
& tho thy thorns withold the may   45
Their shades the violets bring
Which childern stoop for in their play
As tokens of the spring

The time when daiseys bloom divine
With thy calm hours begun   50
& crowflowers blazing blooms are thine
Bright childern of the sun
Along thy woodlands shaded nooks
The primrose wanly comes
& shining in thy pebley brooks   55
The horse bleb gaily blooms

The long lost charm of sparkling dew
Thy gentle birth recieves
& on thy wreathing locks we view
The first infolding leaves   60

[March 1822]

IV

The shepherd on his pasture walks 25
    The first fair cowslip finds,
Whose tufted flowers, on slender stalks,
    Keep nodding to the winds.
And though the thorns withhold the May,
    Their shades the violets bring, 30
Which children stoop for in their play
    As tokens of the Spring.

1827

& seeking firstling buds & flowers
The trials of thy skill
Were pastimes of my infant hours
& so they haunt me still

To see thy first broad arum leaves   65
I lovd them from a child
& were thy woodbines sprouting weaves
I joyd to trace the wild
& jocund as thy lambs at play
I met the wanton wind   70
With feelings that have passed away
Whose shadows cling behind

Those joys which childhood claims its own
Woud they were kin to men
Those treasures to the world unknown   75
When known – was witherd then
But hovering round our growing years
To gild cares sable shroud
Their spirit thro the gloom appears
As suns behind a cloud   80

As thou first met my infant eyes
When thro thy fields I flew
Whose distance were they meet the skyes
Was all the worlds I knew
That warmth of fancys wildest hours   85
Which made things kin to life
That heard a voice in trees & flowers
Has swoond in reasons strife

Sweet month thy pleasures bids thee be
The fairest child of spring   90
& every hour that comes to thee
Comes some new joy to bring

[March 1822]

V

Those joys which childhood calls its own,
    Would they were kin to men!
Those treasures to the world unknown,   35
    When known, are wither'd then!
But hovering round our growing years,
    To gild Care's sable shroud,
Their spirit through the gloom appears
    As suns behind a cloud.   40

VI

Since thou didst meet my infant eyes,
    As through the fields I flew,
Whose distance, where they meet the skies,
    Was all the world I knew;
That warmth of Fancy's wildest hours,   45
    Which fill'd all things with life,
Which heard a voice in trees and flowers,
    Has swoon'd in Reason's strife.

VII

Sweet Month! thy pleasures bid thee be
    The fairest child of Spring;   50
And every hour, that comes with thee,
    Comes some new joy to bring:

1827

The trees still deepen in their bloom
Grass greens the meadow lands
& flowers with every morning come
As dropt by fairey hands   95

The field & gardens lovley hours
Begin & end with thee
For whats so sweet as peeping flowers
& bursting buds to see   100
What time the dews unsullied drops
In burnish gold distills
On crocus flowers unclosing tops
& drooping daffodils

Each day with added glorys come   105
& as they leave the night
Put on the roseys lovley bloom
& blushes with delight
& suns that wait their welcome birth
With earlier haste pursue   110
Their journeys to this lower earth
To free their steps from dew

To see thee come all hearts rejoice
& warms with feelings strong
With thee all nature finds a voice   115
& hums a waking song
The lover views thy welcome hours
& thinks of summer come
& takes the maid thy early flowers
To tempt her steps from home   120

Along each hedge & sprouting bush
The singing birds are blest
& linnet green & speckld thrush
Prepare their mossy nest

[March 1822]

The trees still deepen in their bloom,
    Grass greens the meadow-lands,
And flowers with every morning come, 55
    As dropt by fairy hands.

VIII

The field and garden's lovely hours
    Begin and end with thee;
For what's so sweet, as peeping flowers
    And bursting buds to see, 60
What time the dew's unsullied drops,
    In burnish'd gold, distil
On crocus flowers' unclosing tops,
    And drooping daffodil?

IX

To see thee come, all hearts rejoice; 65
    And, warm with feelings strong,
With thee all Nature finds a voice,
    And hums a waking song.
The lover views thy welcome hours,
    And thinks of summer come, 70
And takes the maid thy early flowers,
    To tempt her steps from home.

X

Along each hedge and sprouting bush
    The singing birds are blest,
And linnet green and speckled thrush 75
    Prepare their mossy nest;

1827

On the warm bed thy plain supplys 125
The young lambs find repose
& mid thy green hills basking lies
Like spots of lingering snows

Young things of tender life again
Enjoys thy sunny hours 130
& gosslings waddle oer the plain
As yellow as its flowers
Or swim the pond in wild delight
To catch the water flye
Were hissing geese in ceasless spite 135
Make childern scamper bye

Again the fairey tribes pursue
Their pleasures on the plain
& brightend with the morning dew
Black circles shine again 140
& on its superstitious ground
Were flowers seem loath to dwell
The toadstools fuzzy balls abou[n]d
& mushrooms yearly swell

The seasons beautys all are thine 145
That visit with the year
Beautys that poets think divine
& all delight to hear
Thy latter days a pleasure brings
That gladden every heart 150
Pleasures that come like lovley things
But like to shades depart

Thy opend leaves & ripend buds
The cuckoo makes his choice
& shepherds in thy greening woods 155
First hears the cheering voice

[March 1822]

On the warm bed thy plains supply,
  The young lambs find repose,
And 'mid thy green hills basking lie
  Like spots of ling'ring snows.   80

XI
Thy open'd leaves and ripen'd buds
  The cuckoo makes his choice,
And shepherds in thy greening woods
  First hear his cheering voice:

1827

& to thy ripend blooming bowers
The nightingale belongs
& singing to thy parting hours
Keeps night awake with songs   160

With thee the swallow dares to come
& prunes his sutty wings
& urgd to seek their yearly home
Thy suns the Martin brings
& lovley month be leisure mine   165
Thy yearly mate to be
Tho may day scenes may brighter shine
Their birth belongs to thee

I waked me with thy rising sun
& thy first glorys viewd   170
& as thy welcome hours begun
Their sunny steps pursued
& now thy sun is on the set
Like to a lovely eve
I view thy parting with regret   175
& linger loath to leave

Thou lovley april fare thee well
Thou early child of spring
Tho born were storms too often dwell
Thy parents news to bring   180
Yet what thy parting youth supplys
No other months excell
Thou first for flowers & sunny skyes
Sweet april fare thee well

[March 1822]

And to thy ripen'd blooming bowers   85
   The nightingale belongs;
And, singing to thy parting hours,
   Keeps night awake with songs!

XII

With thee the swallow dares to come,
   And cool his sultry wing;   90
And, urged to seek his yearly home,
   Thy suns the martin bring.
O! lovely Month! be leisure mine
   Thy yearly mate to be;
Though May-day scenes may brighter shine,   95
   Their birth belongs to thee.

XIII

I waked me with thy rising sun,
   And thy first glories viewed,
And, as thy welcome hours begun,
   Their sunny steps pursued.   100
And now thy sun is on thee set,
   Like to a lovely eve,
I view thy parting with regret,
   And linger loath to leave. –

XIV

Though at her birth the northern gale   105
   Come with its withering sigh;
And hopeful blossoms, turning pale,
   Upon her bosom die;
Ere April seeks another place,
   And ends her reign in this,   110
She leaves us with as fair a face
   As e'er gave birth to bliss!

MAY

MAY

[January/February 1824 – March 1826]

Come queen of months in company
Wi all thy merry mistrelsy
The restless cuckoo absent long
& twittering swallows chimney song
& hedge row crickets notes that run   5
From every bank that fronts the sun
& swathy bees about the grass
That stops wi every bloom they pass
& every minute every hour
Keep teazing weeds that wear a flower   10
& toil & childhoods humming joys
For there is music in the noise
The village childern mad for sport
In school times leisure ever short
That cuck & catch the bouncing ball   15
& run along the church yard wall
Capt wi rude figured slabs whose claims
In times bad memory hath no names
Oft racing round the nookey church
Or calling ecchos in the porch   20
& jelting oer the weather cock
Viewing wi jealous eyes the clock
Oft leaping grave stones leaning hights
Uncheckt wi mellancholy sights
The green grass swelld in many a heap   25
Were kin & friends & parents sleep
Unthinking in their jovial cry
That time shall come when they shall lye
As lonly & as still as they
While other boys above them play   30
Heedless as they do now to know
The unconcous dust that lies below
The shepherd goes wi happy stride
Wi morns long shadow by his side
Down the dryd lanes neath blooming may   35

MAY

1827

COME, Queen of Months! in company
With all thy merry mistrelsy: –
The restless cuckoo, absent long,
And twittering swallows' chimney-song;
With hedgerow crickets' notes, that run   5
From every bank that fronts the sun;
And swarthy bees, about the grass,
That stop with every bloom they pass,
And every minute, every hour,
Keep teazing weeds that wear a flower;   10
And Toil, and Childhood's humming joys!
For there is music in the noise
When village children, wild for sport,
In school-time's leisure, ever short,
Alternate catch the bounding ball;   15
Or run along the church-yard wall,
Capp'd with rude figured slabs, whose claims
In time's bad memory have no names;
Or race around the nooky church;
Or raise loud echoes in the porch;   20
Throw pebbles o'er the weather-cock,
Viewing with jealous eyes the clock;
Or leap o'er grave-stones' leaning heights,
Uncheck'd by melancholy sights,
Though green grass swells in many a heap   25
Where kin, and friends, and parents sleep.
They think not, in their jovial cry,
The time will come, when they shall lie
As lowly and as still as they;
While other boys above them play,   30
Heedless, as they are now, to know
The unconscious dust that lies below.

That once was over shoes in clay
While martins twitter neath his eves
Which he at early morning leaves
The driving boy beside his team
Will oer the may month beauty dream   40
& cock his hat & turn his eye
On flower & tree & deepning skye
& oft bursts loud in fits of song
& whistles as he reels along
Crack[ing] his whip in starts of joy   45
A happy dirty driving boy
The youth who leaves his corner stool
Betimes for neighbouring village school
While as a mark to urge him right
The church spires all the way in sight   50
Wi cheerings from his parents given
Starts neath the joyous smiles of heaven
& sawns wi many an idle stand
Wi bookbag swinging in his hand
& gazes as he passes bye   55
On every thing that meets his eye
Young lambs seem tempting him to play
Dancing & bleating in his way
Wi trembling tails & pointed ears
They follow him & loose their fears   60
He smiles upon their sunny faces
& feign woud join their happy races
The birds that sing on bush & tree
Seem chirping for his company
& all in fancys idle whim   65
Seem keeping holiday but him
He lolls upon each resting stile
To see the fields so sweetly smile
To see the wheat grow green & long
& list the weeders toiling song   70
Or short not[e] of the changing thrush
Above him in the white thorn bush
That oer the leaning stile bends low
Loaded wi mockery of snow
Mozzld wi many a lushy thread   75

[January/February 1824 – March 1826]

The driving boy, beside his team,
Of May-month's beauty now will dream,
And cock his hat, and turn his eye   35
On flower, and tree, and deepening sky;
And oft burst loud in fits of song,
And whistle as he reels along;
Cracking his whip in starts of joy –
A happy, dirty, driving boy.   40
The youth, who leaves his corner stool
Betimes for neighbouring village-school,
Where, as a mark to guide him right,
The church spire's all the way in sight,
With cheerings from his parents given,   45
Beneath the joyous smiles of Heaven
Saunters, with many an idle stand,
With satchel swinging in his hand,
And gazes, as he passes by,
On every thing that meets his eye.   50
Young lambs seem tempting him to play,
Dancing and bleating in his way;
With trembling tails and pointed ears
They follow him, and lose their fears;
He smiles upon their sunny faces,   55
And fain would join their happy races.
The birds, that sing on bush and tree,
Seem chirping for his company; –
And all – in fancy's idle whim –
Seem keeping holiday, but him.   60
He lolls upon each resting stile,
To see the fields so sweetly smile –
To see the wheat grow green and long;
And lists the weeder's toiling song,
Or short note of the changing thrush   65
Above him in the white-thorn bush,
That o'er the leaning stile bends low
Its blooming mockery of snow.

1827

Of crab tree blossoms delicate red
He often bends wi many a wish
Oer the brig rail to view the fish
Go sturting by in sunny gleams
& chucks in the eye dazzld streams   80
Crumbs from his pocket oft to watch
The swarming struttle come to catch
Then were they to the bottom sile
Sighing in fancys joy the while
He s cautiond not to stand so nigh   85
By rosey milkmaid tripping bye
Were he admires wi fond delight
& longs to be their mate till night
He often ventures thro the day
At truant now & then to play   90
Rambling about the field & plain
Seeking larks nests in the grain
& picking flowers & boughs of may
To hurd awhile & throw away
Lurking neath bushes from the sight   95
Of tell tale eyes till schools noon night
Listning each hour for church clocks hum
To know the hour to wander home
That parents may not think him long
Nor dream of his rude doing wrong   100
Dreading thro night wi dreaming pain
To meet his masters wand again
Each hedge is loaded thick wi green
& were the hedger late hath been
Tender shoots begin to grow   105
From the mossy stumps below
While sheep & cow that teaze the grain
Will nip them to the root again
They lay their bill & mittens bye
& on to other labours hie   110
While wood men still on spring intrudes
& thins the shadow[s] solitudes
Wi sharpend axes felling down
The oak trees budding into brown
Were as they crash upon the ground   115

[January/February 1824 – March 1826]

Each hedge is cover'd thick with green;
And where the hedger late hath been,   70
Young tender shoots begin to grow
From out the mossy stumps below.

But woodmen still on Spring intrude,
And thin the shadow's solitude;
With sharpen'd axes felling down   75
The oak-trees budding into brown,
Which, as they crash upon the ground,

1827

A crowd of labourers gather round
& mix among the shadows dark
To rip the crackling staining bark
From off the tree & lay when done
The rolls in lares to meet the sun   120
Depriving yearly were they come
The green wood pecker of its home
That early in the spring began
Far from the sight of troubling man
& bord their round holes in each tree   125
In fancys sweet security
Till startld wi the woodmans noise
It wakes from all its dreaming joys
The blue bells too that thickly bloom
Were man was never feard to come   130
& smell smocks that from view retires
Mong rustling leaves & bowing briars
& stooping lilys of the valley
That comes wi shades & dews to dally
White beading drops on slender threads   135
Wi broad hood leaves above their heads
Like white robd maids in summer hours
Neath umberellas shunning showers
These neath the barkmens crushing treads
Oft perish in their blooming beds   140
Thus stript of boughs & bark in white
Their trunks shine in the mellow light
Beneath the green surviving trees
That wave above them in the breeze
& waking whispers slowly bends   145
As if they mournd their fallen friends
Each morning now the weeders meet
To cut the thistle from the wheat
& ruin in the sunny hours
Full many wild weeds of their flowers   150
Corn poppys that in crimson dwell
Calld "head achs" from their sickly smell
& carlock yellow as the sun
That oer the may fields thickly run
& "iron weed" content to share   155

[January/February 1824 – March 1826]

A crowd of labourers gather round.
These, mixing 'mong the shadows dark,
Rip off the crackling, staining bark;   80

Depriving yearly, when they come,
The green woodpecker of his home,
Who early in the Spring began,
Far from the sight of troubling man,
To bore his round holes in each tree   85
In fancy's sweet security;
Now, startled by the woodman's noise,
He wakes from all his dreary joys.
The blue-bells too, that thickly bloom
Where man was never known to come;   90

And stooping lilies of the valley,
That love with shades and dews to dally,
And bending droop on slender threads,
With broad hood-leaves above their heads,
Like white-robed maids, in summer hours,   95
Beneath umbrellas shunning showers; –
These, from the bark-men's crushing treads,
Oft perish in their blooming beds.
Stripp'd of its boughs and bark, in white
The trunk shines in the mellow light   100
Beneath the green surviving trees,
That wave above it in the breeze,
And, waking whispers, slowly bend,
As if they mourn'd their fallen friend.
     Each morning, now, the weeders meet   105
To cut the thistle from the wheat,
And ruin, in the sunny hours,
Full many a wild weed with its flowers; –
Corn-poppies, that in crimson dwell,
Call'd "Head-achs," from their sickly smell;   110
And charlocks, yellow as the sun,
That o'er the May-fields quickly run;
And "Iron-weed," content to share

1827

The meanest spot that spring can spare
Een roads were danger hourly comes
Is not wi out its purple blooms
& leaves wi pricks like thistles round
Thick set that have no strength to wound   160
That shrink to childhoods eager hold
Like hair – & with its eye of gold
& scarlet starry points of flowers
Pimpernel dreading nights & showers
Oft calld "the shepherds weather glass"   165
That sleep till suns have dryd the grass
Then wakes & spreads its creeping bloom
Till clouds or threatning shadows come
Then close it shuts to sleep again
Which weeders see & talk of rain   170
& boys that mark them shut so soon
Will call them "John go bed at noon"
& fumitory too a name
That superstitition holds to fame
Whose red & purple mottld flowers   175
Are cropt by maids in weeding hours
To boil in water milk & way
For washes on an holiday
To make their beauty fair & sleak
& scour the tan from summers cheek   180
& simple small forget me not
Eyd wi a pinshead yellow spot
I th middle of its tender blue
That gains from poets notice due
These flowers their toil by crowds destroys   185
& robs them of their lonly joys
That met the may wi hopes as sweet
As those her suns in gardens meet
& oft the dame will feel inclind
As childhoods memory comes to mind   190
To turn her hook away & spare
The blooms it lovd to gather there
My wild field catalogue of flowers
Grows in my ryhmes as thick as showers
Tedious & long as they may be   195

[*January/February 1824 – March 1826*]

The meanest spot that Spring can spare –
E'en roads, where danger hourly comes,   115
Are not without its purple blooms,
Whose leaves, with threat'ning thistles round
Thick set, that have no strength to wound,
Shrink into childhood's eager hold
Like hair; and, with its eye of gold   120
And scarlet-starry points of flowers,
Pimpernel, dreading nights and showers,
Oft call'd "the Shepherd's Weather-glass,"
That sleeps till suns have dried the grass,
Then wakes, and spreads its creeping bloom   125
Till clouds with threatening shadows come –
Then close it shuts to sleep again:
Which weeders see, and talk of rain;
And boys, that mark them shut so soon,
Call "John that goes to bed at noon:"   130
And fumitory too – a name
That Superstition holds to fame –
Whose red and purple mottled flowers
Are cropp'd by maids in weeding hours,
To boil in water, milk, and whey,   135
For washes on a holiday,
To make their beauty fair and sleek,
And scare the tan from Summer's cheek;
And simple small "Forget-me-not,"
Eyed with a pin's-head yellow spot   140
I' the middle of its tender blue,
That gains from poets notice due: –
These flowers, that toil by crowds destroys,
Robbing them of their lowly joys,
Had met the May with hopes as sweet   145
As those her suns in gardens meet;
And oft the dame will feel inclined,
As Childhood's memory comes to mind,
To turn her hook away, and spare
The blooms it loved to gather there!   150

1827

To some they never weary me
Then wood & mead & field of grain
I coud hunt oer & oer again
& talk to every blossom wild
Fond as a parent to a child   200
& cull them in my childish joy
By swarms & swarms & never cloy
When their lank shades oer morning pearls
Shrink from their lengths to little girls
& like the clock hand pointing one   205
Is turned & tells the morning gone
They leave their toils for dinners hour
Beneath some hedges bramble bower
& season sweet their savory meals
Wi joke & tale & merry peals   210
Of ancient tunes from happy tongues
While linnets join their fitful songs
Perchd oer their heads in frolic play
Among the tufts of motling may
The young girls whisper things of love   215
& from the old dames hearing move
Oft making "love knotts" in the shade
Of blue green oat or wheaten blade
& trying simple charms & spells
That rural superstition tells   220
They pull the little blossom threads
From out the knopweeds button heads
& put the husk wi many a smile
In their white bosoms for awhile
Who if they guess aright the swain   225
That loves sweet fancys trys to gain
Tis said that ere its lain an hour
Twill blossom wi a second flower
& from her white breasts hankerchief
Bloom as they near had lost a leaf   230
When signs appear that tokens wet
As they are neath the bushes met
The girls are glad wi hopes of play
& harping of the holiday
A hugh blue bird will often swim   235

[January/February 1824 – March 1826]

– Now young girls whisper things of love,
And from the old dames' hearing move;
Oft making "love-knots" in the shade,
Of blue-green oat or wheaten blade;
Or, trying simple charms and spells   155
Which rural Superstition tells,
They pull the little blossom threads
From out the knotweed's button heads,
And put the husk, with many a smile,
In their white bosoms for a while, –   160
Then, if they guess aright the swain
Their loves' sweet fancies try to gain,
'Tis said, that ere it lies an hour,
'Twill blossom with a second flower,
And from their bosom's handkerchief   165
Bloom as it ne'er had lost a leaf.
– But signs appear that token wet,
While they are 'neath the bushes met;
The girls are glad with hopes of play,
And harp upon the holiday: –   170
A high blue bird is seen to swim

1827

Along the wheat when skys grow dim
Wi clouds – slow as the gales of spring
In motion wi dark shadowd wing
Beneath the coming storm it sails
& lonly chirps the wheat hid quails   240
That come to live wi spring again
& start when summer browns the grain
They start the young girls joys afloat
Wi "wet my foot" its yearly note
So fancy doth the sound explain   245
& proves it oft a sign of rain
About the moor mong sheep & cow
The boy or old man wanders now
Hunting all day wi hopful pace
Each thick sown rushy thistly place   250
For plovers eggs while oer them flye
The fearful birds wi teazing cry
Trying to lead their steps astray
& coying him another way
& be the weather chill or warm   255
Wi brown hats truckd beneath his arm
Holding each prize their search has won
They plod bare headed to the sun
Now dames oft bustle from their wheels
Wi childern scampering at their heels   260
To watch the bees that hang & snive
In clumps about each thronging hive
& flit & thicken in the light
While the old dame enjoys the sight
& raps the while their warming pans   265
A spell that superstitition plans
To coax them in the gardens bounds
As if they lovd the tinkling sound
& oft one hears the dinning noise
Which dames believe each swarm decoys   270
Around each village day by day
Mingling in the warmth of may
Sweet scented herbs her skill contrives
To rub the bramble platted hives
Fennels thread leaves & crimpld balm   275

[January/February 1824 – March 1826]

Along the wheat, when skies grow dim
With clouds; slow as the gales of Spring
In motion, with dark-shadow'd wing
Beneath the coming storm he sails: 175
And lonely chirp the wheat-hid quails,
That come to live with Spring again,
But leave when Summer browns the grain;
They start the young girl's joys afloat,
With "wet my foot" – their yearly note: –   180
So fancy doth the sound explain,
And oft it proves a sign of rain!

To scent the new house of the swarm
The thresher dull as winter days
& lost to all that spring displays
Still mid his barn dust forcd to stand
Swings his frail round wi weary hand   280
While oer his head shades thickly creep
& hides the blinking owl asleep
& bats in cobweb corners bred
Sharing till night their murky bed
The sunshine trickles on the floor   285
Thro every crivice of the door
& makes his barn were shadows dwell
As irksome as a prisoners cell
& as he seeks his daily meal
As schoolboys from their tasks will steal   290
He often stands in fond delay
To see the daisey in his way
& wild weeds flowering on the wall
That will his childish sports recall
Of all the joys that came wi spring   295
The twirling top the marble ring
The gingling halfpence hussld up
At pitch & toss the eager stoop
To pick up heads the smuggld plays
Neath hovels upon sabbath days   300
When parson he is safe from view
& clerk sings amen in his pew
The sitting down when school was oer
Upon the threshold by his door
Picking from mallows sport to please   305
Each crumpld seed he calld a cheese
& hunting from the stackyard sod
The stinking hen banes velted pod
By youths vain fancys sweetly fed
Christning them his loaves of bread   310
He sees while rocking down the street
Wi weary hands & crimpling feet
Young childern at the self same games
& hears the self same simple names
Still floating on each happy tongue   315

[*January/February 1824 – March 1826*]

The thresher, dull as winter days,
And lost to all that Spring displays,
Still 'mid his barn-dust forced to stand,   185
Swings round his flail with weary hand;
While o'er his head shades thickly creep,
That hide the blinking owl asleep,
And bats, in cobweb-corners bred,
Sharing till night their murky bed.   190
The sunshine trickles on the floor
Through ev'ry crevice of the door:
This makes his barn, where shadows dwell,
As irksome as a prisoner's cell;
And, whilst he seeks his daily meal,   195
As school-boys from their task will steal,
So will he stand with fond delay
To see the daisy in his way,
Or wild weeds flowering on the wall; –
For these to memory still recall   200
The joys, the sports that come with Spring, –
The twirling top, the marble ring,
The jingling halfpence hustled up
At pitch and toss, the eager stoop
To pick up *heads*, the smuggled plays   205
'Neath hovels upon sabbath-days, –

The sitting down, when school was o'er,
Upon the threshold of the door,
Picking from mallows, sport to please,
Each crumpled seed he call'd a cheese,   210
And hunting from the stack-yard sod
The stinking henbane's belted pod,
By youth's warm fancies sweetly led
To christen them his loaves of bread.
He sees, while rocking down the street   215
With weary hands and crimpling feet,
Young children at the self-same games,
And hears the self-same boyish names
Still floating on each happy tongue:

Touchd wi the simple scene so strong
Tears almost start & many a sigh
Regrets the happiness gone bye
& in sweet natures holiday
His heart is sad while all is gay   320
How lovly now are lanes & balks
For toils & lovers sunday walks
The daisey & the buttercup
For which the laughing child[ern] stoop
A hundred times throughout the day   325
In their rude ramping summer play
So thickly now the pasture crowds
In gold & silver sheeted clouds
As if the drops in april showers
Had woo d the sun & swoond to flowers   330
The brook resumes its summer dresses
Purling neath grass & water cresses
& mint & flag leaf swording high
Their blooms to the unheeding eye
& taper bowbent hanging rushes   335
& horse tail childerns bottle b[r]ushes
& summer tracks about its brink
Is fresh agen were cattle drink
& on its sunny bank the swain
Stretches his idle length again   340
Soon as the sun forgets the day
The moon looks down on the lovly may
& the little star his friend & guide
Travelling together side by side
& the seven stars & charleses wain   345
Hangs smiling oer green woods agen
The heaven rekindles all alive
Wi light the may bees round the hive
Swarm not so thick in mornings eye
As stars do in the evening skye   350
All all are nestling in their joys
The flowers & birds & pasture boys
The fire tail long a stranger comes
To his last summer haunts & homes
To hollow tree & crevisd wall   355

[January/February 1824 – March 1826]

Touch'd with the simple scene so strong, 220
Tears almost start, and many a sigh
Regrets the happiness gone by;
Thus, in sweet Nature's holiday,
His heart is sad while all is gay.
    How lovely now are lanes and balks, 225
For lovers in their Sunday-walks!
The daisy and the butter-cup –
For which the laughing children stoop
A hundred times throughout the day,
In their rude romping Summer play – 230
So thickly now the pasture crowd,
In a gold and silver sheeted cloud,
As if the drops of April showers
Had woo'd the sun, and changed to flowers.
The brook resumes her Summer dresses, 235
Purling 'neath grass and water-cresses,
And mint and flagleaf, swording high
Their blooms to the unheeding eye;

The Summer tracks about its brink
Are fresh again where cattle drink; 240
And on its sunny bank the swain
Stretches his idle length again;
While all that lives enjoys the birth
Of frolic Summer's laughing mirth.

1827

& in the grass the rails odd call
That featherd spirit stops the swain
To listen to his note again
& school boy still in vain retraces
The secrets of his hiding places   360
In the black thorns crowded cops
Thro its varied turns & stops
The nightingale its ditty weaves
Hid in a multitude of leaves
The boy stops short to hear the strain   365
& "sweet jug jug" he mocks again
The yellow hammer builds its nest
By banks were sun beams earliest rest
That drys the dews from off the grass
Shading it from all that pass   370
Save the rude boy wi ferret gaze
That hunts thro evry secret maze
He finds its pencild eggs agen
All streakd wi lines as if a pen
By natures freakish hand was took   375
To scrawl them over like a book
& from these many mozzling marks
The school boy names them "writing larks"
Bum barrels twit on bush & tree
Scarse bigger then a bumble bee   380
& in a white thorns leafy rest
It builds its curious pudding-nest
Wi hole beside as if a mouse
Had built the little barrel house
Toiling full many a lining feather   385
& bits of grey tree moss together
Amid the noisey rooky park
Beneath the firdales branches dark
The little golden crested wren
Hangs up his gluing nest agen   390
& sticks it to the furry leaves
As martins their beneath the eaves
The old hens leave the roost betimes
& oer the garden pailing climbs
To scrat the gardens fresh turnd soil   395

[January/February 1824 – March 1826]

& if unwatchd his craps to spoil
Oft cackling from the prison yard
To peck about the homclose sward
Catching at butterflys & things
Ere they have time to try their wings   400
The cattle feels the breath of may
& kick & toss their heads in play
The ass beneath his bags of sand
Oft jerks the string from leaders hand
& on the road will eager stoop   405
To pick the sprouting thistle up
Oft answering on his weary way
Some distant neighbours sobbing bray
Din[n]ing the ears of driving boy
As if he felt a fit of joy   410
Wi in its pinfold circle left
Of all its company bereft
Starvd stock no longer noising round
Lone in the nooks of foddering ground
Each skeleton of lingering stack   415
By winters tempests beaten black
Nodds upon props or bolt upright
Stands swarthy in the summer light
& oer the green grass seems to lower
Like stump of old time wasted tower   420
All that in winter lookd for hay
Spread from their batterd haunts away
To pick the grass or lye at lare
Beneath the mild hedge shadows there
Sweet month that gives a welcome call   425
To toil & nature & to all
Yet one day mid thy many joys
Is dead to all its sport & noise
Old may day weres thy glorys gone
All fled & left thee every one   430
Thou comst to thy old haunts & homes
Unnoticd as a stranger comes
No flowers are pluckt to hail the[e] now
Nor cotter seeks a single bough
The maids no more on thy sweet morn   435

[January/February 1824 – March 1826]

Awake their thresholds to adorn
Wi dewey flowers – May locks new come
& princifeathers cluttering bloom
& blue bells from the wood land moss
& cowslip cucking balls to toss   440
Above the garlands swinging hight
Hung in the soft eves sober light
These maid & child did yearly pull
By many a folded apron full
But all is past the merry song   445
Of maidens hurrying along
To crown at eve the earliest cow
Is gone & dead & silent now
The laugh raisd at the mawking thorn
Tyd to the cows tail last that morn   450
The kerchief at arms length displayd
Held up by pairs of swain & maid
While others bolted underneath
Bawling loud wi panting breath
"Duck under water" as they ran   455
Alls ended as they near began
While the new thing that took thy place
Wears faded smiles upon its face
& were inclosure has its birth
It spreads a mildew oer her mirth   460
The herd no longer one by one
Goes plodding on her morning way
& garlands lost & sports nigh gone
Leaves her like thee a common day
Yet summer smiles upon thee still   465
Wi natures sweet unalterd will
& at thy births unworshipd hours
Fills her green lap wi swarms of flowers
To crown thee still as thou hast been
Of spring & summers months the queen   470

[January/February 1824 – March 1826]

JUNE

JUNE[12]

[autumn 1823 – January 1826]

Now summer is in flower & natures hum
Is never silent round her sultry bloom
Insects as small as dust are never done
Wi' glittering dance & reeling in the sun
& green wood fly & blossom haunting bee   5
Are never weary of their melody
Round field hedge now flowers in full glory twine
Large bindweed bells wild hop & streakd woodbine
That lift athirst their slender throated flowers
Agape for dew falls & for honey showers   10
These round each bush in sweet disorder run
& spread their wild hues to the sultry sun
Were its silk netting lace on twigs & leaves
The mottld spider at eves leisure weaves
That every morning meet the poets eye   15
Like faireys dew wet dresses hung to dry
The wheat swells into ear & leaves below
The may month wild flowers & their gaudy show
Bright carlock bluecap & corn poppy red
Which in such clouds of colors wid[e]ly spread   20
That at the sun rise might to fancys eye
Seem to reflect the many colord sky
& leverets seat & lark & partridge nest
It leaves a schoolboys height in snugger rest
& oer the weeders labour overgrows   25
Who now in merry groups each morning goes
To willow skirted meads wi fork & rake
The scented hay cocks in long rows to make
Were their old visitors in russet brown
The hay time butterflyes dance up & down   30
& gads that teaze like whasps the timid maid
& drive the herdboys cows to pond & shade
Who when his dogs assistance fails to stop
Is forcd his half made oaten pipes to drop
& start & halloo thro the dancing heat   35

JUNE

1827

Now summer is in flower, and Nature's hum
Is never silent round her bounteous bloom;
Insects, as small as dust, have never done
With glitt'ring dance, and reeling in the sun;
And green wood-fly, and blossom-haunting bee,   5
Are never weary of their melody.
Round field and hedge, flowers in full glory twine,
Large bind-weed bells, wild hop, and streak'd woodbine,
That lift athirst their slender-throated flowers,
Agape for dew-falls, and for honey showers;   10
These o'er each bush in sweet disorder run,
And spread their wild hues to the sultry sun.
The mottled spider, at eve's leisure, weaves
His webs of silken lace on twigs and leaves,
Which ev'ry morning meet the poet's eye,   15
Like fairies' dew-wet dresses hung to dry.
The wheat swells into ear, and hides below
The May-month wild flowers and their gaudy show,

Leaving, a school-boy's height, in snugger rest,
The leveret's seat, and lark, and partridge nest.   20

To keep their gadding tumult from the wheat
Who in their rage will dangers overlook
& leap like hunters oer the pasture brook
Brushing thro blossomd beans in maddening haste
& stroying corn they scarce can stop to taste   40
Labour pursues its toil in weary mood
& feign woud rest wi shadows in the wood
The mowing gangs bend oer the beeded grass
Were oft the gipseys hungry journeying ass
Will turn its wishes from the meadow paths   45
Listning the rustle of the falling swaths
The ploughman sweats along the fallow vales
& down the suncrackt furrow slowly trails
Oft seeking when athirst the brooks supply
Were brushing eager the brinks bushes bye   50
For coolest water he oft brakes the rest
Of ring dove brooding oer its idle nest
& there as loath to leave the swaily place
He'll stand to breath & whipe his burning face
The shepherds idle hours are over now   55
Nor longer leaves him neath the hedgrow bough
On shadow pillowd banks & lolling stile
Wilds looses now their summer friends awhile
Shrill whistles barking dogs & chiding scold
Drive bleating sheep each morn from fallow fold   60
To wash pits were the willow shadows lean
Dashing them in their fold staind coats to clean
Then turnd on sunny sward to dry agen
They drove them homward to the clipping pen
In hurdles pent were elm or sycamore   65
Shut out the sun – or in some threshing floor
There they wi scraps of songs & laugh & tale
Lighten their anual toils while merry ale
Goes round & gladdens old mens hearts to praise
The thread bare customs of old farmers days   70
Who while the sturting sheep wi trembling fears
Lies neath the snipping of his harmless sheers
Recalls full many a thing by bards unsung
& pride forgot – that reignd when he was young
How the hugh bowl was in the middle set   75

[autumn 1823 – January 1826]

The mowers now bend o'er the beaded grass,
Where oft the gipsy's hungry journeying ass
Will turn his wishes from the meadow paths,
List'ning the rustle of the falling swaths.
The ploughman sweats along the fallow vales,   25
And down the sun-crack'd furrow slowly trails;
Oft seeking, when athirst, the brook's supply,
Where, brushing eagerly the bushes by
For coolest water, he disturbs the rest
Of ring-dove, brooding o'er its idle nest.   30

The shepherd's leisure hours are over now;
No more he loiters 'neath the hedge-row bough,
On shadow-pillowed banks and lolling stile;
The wilds must lose their summer friend awhile.
With whistle, barking dogs, and chiding scold,   35
He drives the bleating sheep from fallow fold
To wash-pools, where the willow shadows lean,
Dashing them in, their stained coats to clean;
Then, on the sunny sward, when dry again,
He brings them homeward to the clipping pen,   40
Of hurdles form'd, where elm or sycamore
Shut out the sun – or to some threshing-floor.
There with the scraps of songs, and laugh, and tale,
He lightens annual toil, while merry ale
Goes round, and glads some old man's heart to praise   45
The threadbare customs of his early days:

How the high bowl was in the middle set

1827

At breakfast time as clippers yearly met
Filld full of frumity were yearly swum
The streaking sugar & the spotting plumb
Which maids coud never to the table bring
Without one rising from the merry ring   80
To lend a hand who if twas taen amiss
Woud sell his kindness for a stolen kiss
The large stone pitcher in its homly trim
& clouded pint horn wi its copper rim
Oer which rude healths was drank in spirits high   85
From the best broach the cellar woud supply
While sung the ancient swains in homly ryhmes
Songs that were pictures of the good old times
When leathern bottles held the beer nut brown
That wakd the sun wi songs & sung him down   90
Thus will the old man ancient ways bewail
Till toiling sheers gain ground upon the tale
& brakes it off – when from the timid sheep
The fleece is shorn & wi a fearfull leap
He starts – while wi a pressing hand   95
His sides are printed by the tarry brand
Shaking his naked skin wi wondering joys
& fresh ones are tugd in by sturdy boys
Who when theyre thrown down neath the sheering swain
Will wipe his brow & start his tale again   100
Tho fashions haughty frown hath thrown aside
Half the old forms simpl[i]city supplyd
Yet there are some prides winter deigns to spare
Left like green ivy when the trees are bare
& now when sheering of the flocks are done   105
Some ancient customs mixd wi harmless fun
Crowns the swains merry toils – the timid maid
Pleasd to be praisd & yet of praise affraid
Seeks her best flowers not those of woods & fields
But such as every farmers garden yield[s]   110
Fine cabbage roses painted like her face
& shining pansys trimd in golden lace
& tall tuft larkheels featherd thick wi flowers
& woodbines climbing oer the door in bowers
& London tufts of many a mottld hue   115

[autumn 1823 – January 1826]

At breakfast time, when clippers yearly met,
Fill'd full of furmety, where dainty swum
The streaking sugar and the spotting plum.   50
The maids could never to the table bring
The bowl, without one rising from the ring
To lend a hand; who, if 'twere ta'en amiss,
Would sell his kindness for a stolen kiss.
The large stone pitcher in its homely trim,   55
And clouded pint-horn with its copper rim,
Were there; from which were drunk, with spirits high,
Healths of the best the cellar could supply;
While sung the ancient swains, in uncouth rhymes,
Songs that were pictures of the good old times.   60

Thus will the old man ancient ways bewail,
Till toiling shears gain ground upon the tale,
And break it off – for now the timid sheep,
His fleece shorn off, starts with a fearful leap,

Shaking his naked skin with wond'ring joys,   65
While others are brought in by sturdy boys.

   Though fashion's haughty frown hath thrown aside
Half the old forms simplicity supplied,
Yet there are some pride's winter deigns to spare,
Left like green ivy when the trees are bare.   70
And now, when shearing of the flocks is done,
Some ancient customs, mix'd with harmless fun,
Crown the swain's merry toils. The timid maid,
Pleased to be praised, and yet of praise afraid,
Seeks the best flowers; not those of woods and fields,   75
But such as every farmer's garden yields –
Fine cabbage-roses, painted like her face;
The shining pansy, trim'd with golden lace;
The tall topp'd larkheels, feather'd thick with flowers;
The woodbine, climbing o'er the door in bowers;   80
The London tufts, of many a mottled hue;

1827

& pale pink pea & monkshood darkly blue
& white & purple jiliflowers that stay
Lingering in blossom summer half away
& single blood walls of a lucious smell
Old fashiond flowers which huswives love so well   120
& columbines stone blue or deep night brown
Their honey-comb-like blossoms hanging down
Each cottage gardens fond adopted child
Tho heaths still claim them were they yet grow wild
Mong their old wild companions summer blooms   125
Furze brake & mozzling ling & golden broom
Snap dragons gaping like to sleepy clowns
& "clipping pinks" (which maidens sunday gowns
Full often wear catcht at by toying chaps)
Pink as the ribbons round their snowy caps   130
"Bess in her bravery" too of glowing dyes
As deep as sunsets crimson pillowd skyes
& majoram notts sweet briar & ribbon grass
& lavender the choice of every lass
& sprigs of lads love all familiar names   135
Which every garden thro the village claims
These the maid gathers wi a coy delight
& tyes them up in readiness for night
Giving to every swain tween love & shame
Her "clipping poseys" as their yearly claim   140
& turning as he claims the custom kiss
Wi stifld smiles half ankering after bliss
She shrinks away & blushing calls it rude
But turns to smile & hopes to be pursued
While one to whom the seeming hint applied   145
Follows to claim it & is not denyd
No doubt a lover for within his coat
His nosgay owns each flower of better sort
& when the envious mutter oer their beer
& nodd the secret to his neighbor near   150
Raising the laugh to make the matter known
She blushes silent & will not disown
& ale & songs & healths & merry ways
Keeps up a shadow of old farmers days
But the old beachen bowl that once supplyd   155

[autumn 1823 – January 1826]

The pale pink pea, and monkshood darkly blue;
The white and purple gilliflowers, that stay
Ling'ring, in blossom, summer half away;
The single blood-walls, of a luscious smell,   85
Old-fashion'd flowers which housewives love so well;
The columbines, stone-blue, or deep night-brown,
Their honeycomb-like blossoms hanging down,
Each cottage-garden's fond adopted child,
Though heaths still claim them, where they yet grow wild;   90

With marjoram knots, sweet-brier, and ribbon-grass,
And lavender, the choice of ev'ry lass,
And sprigs of lad's-love – all familiar names,
Which every garden through the village claims.
These the maid gathers with a coy delight,   95
And ties them up, in readiness for night;
Then gives to ev'ry swain, 'tween love and shame,
Her "clipping posies" as his yearly claim.
He rises, to obtain the custom'd kiss: –
With stifled smiles, half hankering after bliss,   100
She shrinks away, and blushing, calls it rude;
Yet turns to smile, and hopes to be pursued;
While one, to whom the hint may be applied,
Follows to claim it, and is not denied.

The rest the loud laugh raise, to make it known, –   105
She blushes silent, and will not disown!
Thus ale, and song, and healths, and merry ways,
Keep up a shadow still of former days;
But the old beechen bowl, that once supplied

1827

Its feast of frumity is thrown aside
& the old freedom that was living then
When masters made them merry wi their men
Whose coat was like his neighbors russet brown
& whose rude speech was vulgar as his clown   160
Who in the same horn drank the rest among
& joind the chorus while a labourer sung
All this is past – & soon may pass away
The time torn remnant of the holiday
As proud distinction makes a wider space   165
Between the genteel & the vulgar race
Then must they fade as pride oer custom showers
Its blighting mildew on her feeble flowers

[autumn 1823 – January 1826]

The feast of furmety, is thrown aside;   110
And the old freedom that was living then,
When masters made them merry with their men;
When all their coats alike were russet brown,
And his rude speech was vulgar as their own –

All this is past, and soon may pass away   115
The time-torn remnant of the holiday.

JULY

JULY[13]

[February 1826]

July the month of summers prime
Again resumes her busy time
Scythes tinkle in each grassy dell
Where solitude was wont to dwell
& meadows they are mad with noise 5
Of laughing maids & shouting boys
Making up the withering hay
With merry hearts as light as play
The very insects on the ground
So nimbly bustle all around 10
Among the grass or dusty soil
They seem partakers in the toil
The very landscap reels with life
While mid the busy stir & strife
Of industry the shepherd still 15
Enjoys his summer dreams at will
Bent oer his hook or listless laid
Beneath the pastures willow shade
Whose foliage shines so cool & grey
Amid the sultry hues of day 20
As if the mornings misty veil
Yet lingered in their shadows pale
Or lolling in a musing mood
On mounds were saxon[14] castles stood
Upon whose deeply buried walls 25
The ivyed oaks dark shadow falls
Oft picking up with wondering gaze
Some little thing of other days
Saved from the wreck of time – as beads
Or broken pots among the weeds 30
Of curious shapes – & many a stone
Of roman pavements thickly sown
Oft hoping as he searches round
That buried riches may be found
Tho search as often as he will 35

JULY

1827

JULY, the month of Summer's prime,
Again resumes his busy time;
Scythes tinkle in each grassy dell,
Where solitude was wont to dwell;
And meadows, they are mad with noise   5
Of laughing maids and shouting boys,
Making up the withering hay
With merry hearts as light as play.
The very insects on the ground
So nimbly bustle all around,   10
Among the grass, or dusty soil,
They seem partakers in the toil.
The landscape even reels with life,
While 'mid the busy stir and strife
Of industry, the shepherd still   15
Enjoys his summer dreams at will;
Bent o'er his book, or listless laid
Beneath the pasture's willow shade,
Whose foliage shines so cool and gray
Amid the sultry hues of day,   20
As if the morning's misty veil
Yet linger'd in its shadows pale;
Or lolling in a musing mood
On mounds where Saxon castles stood,
Upon whose deeply-buried walls   25
The ivy'd oak's dark shadow falls,
He oft picks up with wond'ring gaze
Some little thing of other days,
Saved from the wrecks of time – as beads,
Or broken pots among the weeds,   30
Of curious shapes – and many a stone
From Roman pavements thickly strown,
Oft hoping, as he searches round,
That buried riches may be found,
Though, search as often as he will,   35

His hopes are dissapointed still
& marking oft upon his seat
The insect world beneath his feet
In busy motion here & there
Like visitors to feast or fair   40
Some climbing up the rushes stem
A steeples height or more to them
With speed that sees no fear to drop
Till perched upon its spirey top
Where they awhile the view survey   45
Then prune their wings & flit away
Others journeying too & fro
Throng the grassy woods below
Musing as if they felt & knew
The pleasant scenes they wandered thro   50
Where each bent round them seems to be
A hugh & massive timber tree
While pismires from their castles come
In crowds to seek the litterd crumb
Which he on purpose drops that they   55
May hawl the heavy loads away
Shaping the while their dark employs
To his own visionary joys
Picturing such a life as theirs
As free from summers sweating cares   60
& inly wishing that his own
Coud meet with joys so thickly sown
He thinks sport all that they pursue
& play the all they have to do
The cowboy still cuts short the day   65
Mingling mischief with his play
Oft in the pond with weeds oergrown
Hurling quick the plashing stone
To cheat his dog who watching lies
& instant plunges for the prize   70
& tho each effort proves as vain
He shakes his coat & dives again
Till wearied with the fruitless play
Then drops his tail & sneaks away
Nor longer heeds the bawling boy   75

[February 1826]

His hopes are disappointed still;
Or watching, on his mossy seat,
The insect world beneath his feet,
In busy motion here and there
Like visitors to feast or fair,   40
Some climbing up the rush's stem,
A steeple's height or more to them,
With speed, that sees no fear to stop,
Till perch'd upon its spiry top,
Where they awhile the view survey,   45
Then prune their wings, and flit away, –
And others journeying to and fro
Among the grassy woods below,
Musing, as if they felt and knew
The pleasant scenes they wander'd through,   50
Where each bent round them seems to be
Huge as a giant timber-tree.

Shaping the while their dark employs
To his own visionary joys,
He pictures such a life as their's,   55
As free from Summer's sultry cares,
And only wishes that his own
Could meet with joys so thickly sown:
Sport seems the all that they pursue,
And play the only work they do.   60
    The cow-boy still cuts short the day,
By mingling mischief with his play;
Oft in the pond, with weeds o'ergrown,
Hurling quick the plashing stone
To cheat his dog, who watching lies,   65
And instant plunges for the prize;
And though each effort proves in vain,
He shakes his coat, and dives again,
Till, wearied with the fruitless play,
He drops his tail, and sneaks away,   70
Nor longer heeds the bawling boy,

1827

Who seeks new sports with added joy
& on some banks oer hanging brow
Beats the whasps nest with a bough
Till armys from the hole appear
& threaten vengance in his ear   80
With such determined hue & cry
As makes the bold besiegers flye
Elsewere fresh mischief to renew
& still his teazing sports pursue
Pelting with excessive glee   85
The squirrel on the wood land tree
Who nimbles round from grain to grain
& cocks his tail & peeps again
Half pleased as if he thought the fray
Which mischief made was meant for play   90
Till scared & startled into flight
He instant huries out of sight
Thus he his leisure hour employs
& feeds on busy meddling joys
While in the willow shaded pool   95
His cattle stand their hides to cool
Loud is the summers busy song
The smalles[t] breeze can find a tongue
Were insects of each tiney size
Grow teazing with their melodys   100
Till noon burns with its blistering breath
Around & day dyes still as death
The busy noise of man & brute
Is on a sudden lost & mute
The cuckoo singing as she flies   105
No more to mocking boy replys
Even the brook that leaps along
Seems weary of its bubbling song
& so soft its waters creep
Tired silence sinks in sounder sleep   110
The cricket on its banks is dumb
The very flies forget to hum
& save the waggon rocking round
The lanscape sleeps without a sound
The breeze is stopt the lazy bough   115

[February 1826]

Who seeks new sports with added joy:
Now on some bank's o'erhanging brow
Beating the wasp's nest with a bough,
Till armies from the hole appear, 75
And threaten vengeance in his ear
With such determined hue-and-cry
As makes the bold besieger fly;

Then, pelting with excessive glee
The squirrel on the woodland-tree, 80
Who nimbles round from grain to grain,
And cocks his tail, and peeps again,
Half-pleased, as if he thought the fray
Which mischief made, was meant for play,
Till scared and startled into flight, 85
He instant tumbles out of sight.
Thus he his leisure hour employs,
And feeds on busy meddling joys,
While in the willow-shaded pool
His cattle stand, their hides to cool. 90
   Loud is the Summer's busy song,
The smallest breeze can find a tongue,
While insects of each tiny size
Grow teazing with their melodies,
Till noon burns with its blistering breath 95
Around, and day dies still as death.
The busy noise of man and brute
Is on a sudden lost and mute;

Even the brook that leaps along
Seems weary of its bubbling song, 100
And, so soft its waters creep,
Tired silence sinks in sounder sleep.
The cricket on its banks is dumb,
The very flies forget to hum;
And, save the waggon rocking round, 105
The landscape sleeps without a sound.
The breeze is stopt, the lazy bough

Hath not a leaf that dances now
The totter grass upon the hill
& spiders threads are standing still
The feathers dropt from more hens wing
Which to the waters surface cling   120
Are stedfast & as heavy seem
As stones beneath them in the stream
Hawkweeds & Groundsells fanning downs
Unruffled keep their seedy crowns
& in the oven heated air   125
Not one light thing is floating there
– Save that to the earnest eye
The restless heat seems twittering bye
Noon swoons beneath the heat it made
& flowers een wither in the shade   130
Untill the sun slopes in the west
Like weary traveler glad to rest
On pillard clouds of many hues
Then natures voice its joy renews
& checkerd field & grassy plain   135
Hum with their summer songs again
A requiem to the days decline
Whose setting sun beams cooly shine
As welcome to days feeble powers
As evening dews on thirsty flowers   140
Now to the pleasant pasture dells
Where hay from closes sweetly smells
Adown the pathways narrow lane
The milking maiden hies again
With scraps of ballads never dumb   145
& rosey cheeks of happy bloom
Tanned brown by sumers rude embrace
That adds new beautys to her face
& red lips never paled with sighs
& flowing hair & laughing eyes   150
That oer full many a heart prevailed
& swelling bosom loosly veiled
White as the love it harbours there
Unsullied with the taints[15] of care
The mower gives his labour oer   155

[February 1826]

Hath not a leaf that dances now;
The tottergrass upon the hill,
And spiders' threads, are standing still;   110
The feathers dropt from moorhen's wing,
Which to the water's surface cling,
Are steadfast, and as heavy seem
As stones beneath them in the stream;
Hawkweed and groundsel's fanning downs   115
Unruffled keep their seedy crowns;
And in the oven-heated air,
Not one light thing is floating there,
Save that to the earnest eye,
The restless heat seems twittering by.   120
Noon swoons beneath the heat it made,
And flowers e'en wither in the shade,
Until the sun slopes in the west,
Like weary traveller, glad to rest,
On pillowed clouds of many hues;   125
Then nature's voice its joy renews,
And chequer'd field and grassy plain
Hum, with their summer songs again,
A requiem to the day's decline,
Whose setting sunbeams coolly shine,   130
As welcome to day's feeble powers
As falling dews to thirsty flowers.
   Now to the pleasant pasture dells,
Where hay from closes sweetly smells,
Adown the pathway's narrow lane   135
The milking maiden hies again,
With scraps of ballads never dumb,
And rosy cheeks of happy bloom,
Tann'd brown by Summer's rude embrace,
Which adds new beauties to her face,   140
And red lips never pale with sighs,
And flowing hair, and laughing eyes
That o'er full many a heart prevail'd,
And swelling bosom loosely veiled,
White as the love it harbours there,   145
Unsullied with the taunts of care.
   The mower now gives labour o'er,

1827

& on his bench beside the door
Sits down to see his childern play
Or smokes his leisure hour away
While from her cage the black bird sings
That on the wood bine arbour hings   160
& all with quiet joys recieve
The welcom of a summers eve

[February 1826]

And on his bench beside the door
Sits down to see his children play,
Smoking a leisure hour away: 150
While from her cage the blackbird sings,
That on the woodbine arbour hings;
And all with soothing joys receive
The quiet of a Summer's eve.

AUGUST

August[16]

[February/April 1824 – February 1826]

Harvest approaches with its busy day
The wheat tans brown & barley bleaches grey
In yellow garb the oat land intervenes
& tawney glooms the valley thronged with beans
Silent the village grows wood wandering dreams   5
Seem not so lonely as its quiet seems
Doors are shut up as on a winters day
& not a child about them lies at play
The dust that winnows neath the breezes feet
Is all that stirs about the silent street   10
Fancy might think that desert spreading fear
Had whisperd terrors into quiets ear
Or plundering armys past the place had come
& drove the lost inhabitants from home
The fields now claim them where a motley crew   15
Of old & young their daily tasks pursue
The reapers leave their rest before the sun
& gleaners follow in the toils begun
To pick the littered ear the reaper leaves
& glean in open fields among the sheaves   20
The ruddy child nursed in the lap of care
In toils rude strife to do its little share
Beside its mother poddles oer the land
Sun burnt & stooping with a weary hand
Picking its tiney glean of corn or wheat   25
While crackling stubbles wound its little feet
Full glad it often is to sit awhile
Upon a smooth green baulk to ease its toil
& feign would spend an idle hour to play
With insects strangers to the moiling day   30
Creeping about each rush & grassy stem
& often wishes it was one of them
In weariness of heart that it might lye
Hid in the grass from the days burning eye
That raises tender blisters on its skin   35

AUGUST

1827

HARVEST approaches with its busy day;
The wheat tans brown, and barley bleaches grey;
In yellow garb the oatland intervenes,
And tawny glooms the valley throng'd with beans.
Silent the village grows, – wood-wandering dreams   5
Seem not so lonely as its quiet seems;
Doors are shut up as on a winter's day,
And not a child about them lies at play;
The dust that winnows 'neath the breeze's feet
Is all that stirs about the silent street: 10
Fancy might think that desert-spreading Fear
Had whisper'd terrors into Quiet's ear,
Or plundering armies past the place had come
And drove the lost inhabitants from home.
The fields now claim them, where a motley crew   15
Of old and young their daily tasks pursue.
The reapers leave their rest before the sun,
And gleaners follow in the toils begun
To pick the litter'd ear the reaper leaves,
And glean in open fields among the sheaves.   20
The ruddy child, nursed in the lap of Care,
In Toil's rude strife to do its little share,
Beside its mother poddles o'er the land,
Sunburnt, and stooping with a weary hand,
Picking its tiny glean of corn or wheat,   25
While crackling stubbles wound its little feet.
Full glad it often is to sit awhile
Upon a smooth green bank to ease its toil,
And fain would spend an idle hour in play
With insects, strangers to the moiling day,   30
Creeping about each rush and grassy stem,
And often wishes it were one of them:

Thro holes or openings that have lost a pin
Free from the crackling stubs to toil & glean
& smiles to think how happy it had been
Whilst its expecting mother stops to tye
Her handful up & waiting its supply 40
Misses the idle younker from her side
& shouts of rods & morts of threats beside
Picturing harsh truths in its unpracticed eye
How they who idle in the harvest lye
Shall well deserving in the winter pine 45
Or hunt the hedges with the birds & swine
In vain he wishes that the rushes height
Were tall as trees to hide him from her sight
Leaving his pleasant seat he sighs & rubs
His legs & shows scratchd wounds from piercing stubs 50
To make excuse for play but she disdains
His little wounds & smiles while he complains
& as he stoops adown in troubles sore
She sees his grief & bids him mourn no more
As bye & bye on the next sabbath day 55
She'll give him well earned pence as well as play
When he may buy almost with out a stint
Sweet candied horehound cakes & pepper mint
At the gay shop within whose window lyes
Things of all sorts to tempt his eager eyes 60
Rich sugar plumbs in phials shining bright
In every hue young fancys to delight
Coaches & ladys of gilt ginger bread
& downy plumbs & apples streaked with red
Such promises all sorrows soon displace 65
& smiles are instant kindled in his face
Scorning all troubles which he felt before
He picks the trailing ears & mourns no more
    The fields are all alive with sultry noise
Of labours sounds & insects busy joys 70
The reapers oer their glittering sickles stoop
Startling full oft the partridge conveys up
Some oer the rustling scythe go bending on
& shockers follow where their toils have gone
Reaping the swaths that rustle in the sun 75

[February/April 1824 – February 1826]

Meanwhile the expecting mother stops to tie
Her handful up, and, waiting his supply,
Misses the idle younker from her side;   35
Then shouts of rods, and morts of threats beside
Picture harsh truths in his unpractised breast, –
How they, who idle in the harvest rest,
Shall well-deserving in the winter pine,
Or hunt the hedges with the birds and swine.   40
In vain he wishes that the rushes' height
Were tall as trees to hide him from her sight.
Leaving his pleasant seat, he sighs and rubs
His legs, and shows scatch'd wounds from piercing stubs,
To make excuse for play; but she disdains   45
His little wounds, and smiles while he complains;
And as he stoops adown in troubles sore,
She sees his grief, and bids him mourn no more,
For by and by, on the next Sabbath-day,
He shall have well-earn'd pence as well as play,   50
When he may buy, almost without a stint,
Sweet candied horehound, cakes, and peppermint,
At the gay shop, within whose window lie
Things of all sorts to tempt his eager eye:
Rich sugar-plums in phials shining bright,   55
In every hue, young fancies to delight;
Coaches and ladies of gilt gingerbread;
And downy plums, and apples streak'd with red.
Such promises all sorrow soon displace,
And smiles are instant kindled in his face;   60
Scorning the troubles which he felt before,
He picks the trailing ears, and mourns no more.
    The fields are all alive with sultry noise
Of labour's sounds, and insects' busy joys.
The reapers o'er their glittering sickles stoop,   65
Startling full oft the partridge coveys up;
Some o'er the rustling scythe go bending on;
And shockers follow where their toils have gone,
Heaping the swaths that rustle in the sun,

Where mice from terrors dangers nimbly run
Leaving their tender young in fears alarm
Lapt up in nest of chimbled grasses warm
Hoping for safty from their flight in vain
While the rude boy or churlish hearted swain   80
Pursue with lifted weapons oer the ground
& spread an instant murder all around
Tho oft the anxious maidens tender prayer
Urges the clown their little lives to spare
Who sighs while trailing the long rake along   85
At scenes so cruel & forgets her song
When the sun stoops to meet the western sky
& noons hot hours have wanderd weary bye
They seek an awthorn bush or willow tree
For resting places that the coolest be   90
Where baskets heapd & unbroached bottles lye
Which dogs in absence watchd with wary eye
To catch their breath awhile & share the boon
Which beavering time alows their toil at noon
All gathering sit on stubbs or sheaves the hour   95
Where scarlet poppys linger still in flower
   Next to her favoured swain the maiden steals
Blushing at kindness which his love reveals
Who makes a seat for her of things around
& drops beside her on the naked ground   100
Then from its cool retreat the beer they bring
& hand the stout hooped bottle round the ring
Each swain soaks hard – the maiden ere she sips
Shreaks at the bold whasp settling on her lips
That seems determined only hers to greet   105
As if it fancied they were cherrys sweet
The dog forgoes his sleep awhile or play
Springing at frogs that rustling jump away
To watch each morsel that the boon bestows
& wait the bone or crust the shepherd throws   110
For shepherds are no more of ease possest
But share the harvests labours with the rest
When day declines & labour meets repose
The bawling boy his evening journey goes
At toils unwearied call the first & last   115

[February/April 1824 – February 1826]

Where mice from Terror's dangers nimbly run,   70
Leaving their tender young in fear's alarm,
Lapt up in nests of chimbled grasses warm,
Hoping for safety from their flight in vain;
While the rude boy, or churlish-hearted swain,
Pursues with lifted weapons o'er the ground,   75
And spreads an instant murder all around.
In vain the anxious maiden's tender prayer
Urges the clown their little lives to spare;
She sighs, while trailing the long rake along,
At scenes so cruel, and forgets her song.   80
    When the Sun stoops to meet the western sky,
And Noon's hot hours have wander'd weary by,
Seeking a hawthorn bush or willow-tree
For resting-places that the coolest be,
Where baskets heaped and unbroached bottles lie,   85
Which dogs in absence watch'd with wary eye,
They catch their breath awhile, and share the boon
Which bevering-time allows their toil at noon.

Next to her favour'd swain the maiden steals,
Blushing at kindness which his love reveals;   90
Making a seat for her of sheaves around,
He drops beside her on the naked ground.
Then from its cool retreat the beer they bring,
And hand the stout-hoop'd bottle round the ring.
Each swain soaks hard; the maiden, ere she sips,   95
Shrieks at the bold wasp settling on her lips,
That seems determined only her's to greet,
As if it fancied they were cherries sweet!
The dog foregoes his sleep awhile, or play,
Springing at frogs that rustling jump away,   100
To watch each morsel carelessness bestows,
Or wait the bone or crust the shepherd throws;
For shepherds are no more of ease possest,
But share in harvest-labours with the rest.
    When day declines and others meet repose,   105
The bawling boy his evening journey goes;
At toil's unwearied call the first and last,

1827

He drives his horses to their nights repast
In dewey close or meadow to sojourn
& often ventures on his still return
Oer garden pales or orchard walls to hie
When sleeps safe key hath locked up dangers eye   120
All but the mastiff watching in the dark
Who snuffts & knows him & forbears to bark
With fearful haste he climbs each loaded tree
& picks for prizes which the ripest be
Pears plumbs or filberts covered oer in leams   125
While the pale moon creeps high in peaceful dreams
& oer his harvest theft in jealous light
Fills empty shadows with the power to fright
& owlet screaming as it bounces nigh
That from some barn hole pops & hurries bye   130
He hears the noise & trembling to escape
While every object grows a dismal shape
Drops from the tree in fancys swiftest dread
& thinks ghosts with him till he goes to bed
Quick tumbling oer the mossy mouldering wall   135
& looses half his booty in the fall
Where soon as ere the morning opes its eyes
The restless hogs will happen on the prize
& crump adown the mellow & the green
& makes all seem as nothing neer had been   140
     Amid the broils of harvests weary reign
How sweet the sabbath wakes its rest again
& on each weary mind what rapture dwells
To hear once more its pleasant chiming bells
That from each steeple peeping here & there   145
Murmur a soothing lullaby to care
The shepherd journying on his morning rounds
Pauses awhile to hear their pleasing sounds
While the glad childern free from toils employ
Mimic the ding dong sounds & laugh for joy   150
The fields themselves seem happy to be free
Where insects chatter with unusual glee
While solitude the stubbs & grass among
Appears to muse & listen to the song
In quiet peace awakes the welcome morn   155

[February/April 1824 – February 1826]

He drives his horses to their night's repast,
In dewy close or meadow to sojourn;
And often ventures, on his still return,   110
O'er garden pales, or orchard walls, to hie,
When sleep's safe key hath lock'd up danger's eye,
All but the mastiff watching in the dark,
Who snuffs and knows him, and forbears to bark.
With fearful haste he climbs each loaded tree,   115
And picks for prizes, that the ripest be;

While the pale moon, creeping with jealous light,
Fills empty shadows with the power to fright;
And, from the barn-hole, pops and hurries by,
The grey owl, screaming with a fearful cry; –   120
He hears the noise, and, hastening to escape,
Thinks each thing grows around a dismal shape.

Quick tumbling o'er the mossy, mould'ring wall,
He loses half his booty in the fall;
Where, soon as ever Morning opes its eyes,   125
The restless hogs will happen on the prize,
And crump adown the mellow and the green,
Making all seem as nothing e'er had been.
     Amid the broils of harvest's weary reign,
How sweet the Sabbath wakes its rest again!   130
And on each weary mind what rapture dwells,
To hear once more the pleasant chiming bells,
That from each steeple, peeping here and there,
Murmur a soothing lullaby to care.
The shepherd, journeying on his morning rounds,   135
Pauses awhile to hear the pleasing sounds,
While the glad children, free from toil's employ,
Mimic the "ding dong" hums, and laugh for joy.
The fields themselves seem happy to be free,
Where insects chatter with unusual glee;   140
While Solitude, the grass and stubs among,
Appears to muse and listen to the song.
In quiet peace awakes the welcome morn;

Men tired & childern with their gleaning worn
Weary & stiff lye round the doors the day
To rest themselves with little heart for play
No more keck horns in homestead close resounds
As in their school boy days at hare & hounds   160
Nor running oer the street from wall to wall
With eager shouts at 'cuck & catch the ball'
In calm delight the sabbath wears along
Yet round the cross at noon a tempted throng
Of little younkers with their pence repair   165
To buy the downy plumb & lucious pear
That melt i'th mouth – which gardners never fail
For gains strong impulse to expose for sale
& on the circling cross steps in the sun
Sit when the parson has his sermon done   170
When gardners that against his rules rebell
Come wi their baskets heapd wi fruit to sell
That thither all the season did pursue
Wi mellow goos berrys of every hue
Green ruffs & raspberry reds & drops of gold   175
That makes mouths water often to behold
Sold out to clowns in totts oft deemd too small
Who grudging much the price eat husks & all
Nor leaves a fragment round to cheer the eye
Of searching swine that murmurs hungry bye   180
& currans red & white on cabbage leaves
While childerns fingers itches to be thieves
& black red cherrys shining to the sight
As rich as brandy held before the light
Now these are past he still as sunday comes   185
Sits on the cross wi baskets heapd wi plumbs
& Jenitens streakd apples suggar sweet
Others spice scented ripening wi the wheat
& pears that melt ith' mouth like honey which
He oft declares to make their spirits itch   190
They are so juicy ripe & better still
So rich they een might suck em thro a quill
Here at their leisure gather many a clown
To talk of grain & news about the town
& [h]ere the boy wi toils earnd penny comes   195

[February/April 1824 – February 1826]

Men tired, and children with their gleaning worn,
Weary and stiff, lie round the doors all day,   145
To rest themselves, with little heart for play.

In calm delight, the Sabbath wears along;
Yet round the Cross, at noon, a tempted throng
Of little younkers, with their pence, repair
To buy the downy plum and luscious pear   150
That melts i' th' mouth, which gardeners never fail,
For gain's strong impulse, to expose for sale;
Placed on the circling Cross-steps in the sun,
What time the parson has his sermon done.

There, soon the boy his sore-earn'd penny spends;   155

In hurrying speed to purchase pears or plumbs
& oer the basket hangs wi many a smile
Wi hat in hand to hold his prize the while
   No so the boys that begs for pence in vain
Of deaf eard dames that threat while they complain   200
Who talk of the good dinners they have eat
& wanting more as nothing but consiet
Vowing they near shall throw good pence away
So bids them off & be content wi play
Reaching her rod that hangs the chimney oer   205
& scaring their rude whinings to the door
Who sob aloud & hang their hats adown
To hide their tears & sawn along the town
Venturing wi sullen step his basket nigh
& often dipping a desiring eye   210
Stone hearted dames thrifts errors to believe
To make their little bellys yearn to thieve
But strong temptation must to fears resign
For close beside the stocks in terror shine
So choaking substitutes for loss of pelf   215
He keeps his longing fingers to himself
& mopes & sits the sabbath hours away
Wi heart too weary & too sad for play
So sundays scenes & leisure passes bye
In rests soft peace & home tranquillity   220
Till monday morning doth its cares pursue
& wakes the harvests busy toils anew

[February/April 1824 – February 1826]

And he the while, that pennyless attends,

In sullen, silent mood, approaching nigh,
Full often drops a keen, desiring eye,
Upon each loaded basket, to perceive,
What makes his little fingers itch to thieve; –   160
But, close at hand, the stocks in terror shine,
And temptings strong, to stronger fears resign.

Thus Sunday's leisure passes swiftly by
In rest, soft peace, and home-tranquillity,
Till Monday morning doth its cares pursue,   165
Rousing the harvest's busy toils anew.

1827

SEPTEMBER

SEPTEMBER

[February 1826]

Harvest awakes the morning still
& toils rude groups the valleys fill
Deserted is each cottage hearth
To all life save the crickets mirth
Each burring wheel their sabbath meets   5
Nor walks a gossip in the streets
The bench beneath its eldern bough
Lined oer with grass is empty now
Where black birds caged from out the sun
Would whistle while their mistress spun   10
    All haunt the thronged fields still to share
The harvests lingering bounty there
As yet no meddling boys resort
About the streets in idle sport
The butterflye enjoys his hour   15
& flirts unchaced from flower to flower
& humming bees that morning calls
From out the low huts mortar walls
Which passing boy no more controuls
Flye undisturbed about their holes   20
& sparrows in glad chirpings meet
Unpelted in the quiet street
    None but imprison'd childern now
Are seen where dames with angry brow
Threaten each younker to his seat   25
That thro' the school door eyes the street
Or from his horn book turns away
To mourn for liberty & play
    Loud are the mornings early sounds
That farm & cottage yard surrounds   30
The creaking noise of opening gate
& clanking pumps where boys await
With idle motion to supply
The thirst of cattle crowding bye
The low of cows & bark of dogs   35

September

1827

Harvest awakes the morning still,
And toil's rude groups the valleys fill;
Deserted is each cottage hearth
To all life, save the cricket's mirth;
Each burring wheel its sabbath meets,　　　　　5
Nor walks a gossip in the streets;
The bench beneath the eldern bough,
Lined o'er with grass, is empty now,
Where blackbirds, caged from out the sun,
Would whistle while their mistress spun:　　　　10
All haunt the thronged fields, to share
The harvest's lingering bounty there.
　　As yet, no meddling boys resort
About the streets in idle sport;
The butterfly enjoys its hour,　　　　　15
And flirts, unchased, from flower to flower;
The humming bees, which morning calls
From out the low hut's mortar walls,
And passing boy no more controls –
Fly undisturb'd about their holes;　　　　20
The sparrows in glad chirpings meet,
Unpelted in the quiet street.
None but imprison'd children now
Are seen, where dames with angry brow
Threaten each younker to his seat,　　　　25
Who, through the window, eyes the street;
Or from his hornbook turns away,
To mourn for liberty and play.
　　Yet loud are morning's early sounds;
The farm or cottage yard abounds　　　　30
With creaking noise of opening gate,
And clanking pumps, where boys await
With idle motion, to supply
The thirst of cattle crowding nigh.

& cackling hens & wineing hogs
Swell high – while at the noise awoke
Old goody seeks her milking cloak
& hastens out to milk the cow
& fill the troughs to feed the sow   40
Or seeking old hens laid astray
Or from young chickens drives away
The circling kite that round them flyes
Waiting the chance to seize the prize
Hogs trye thro gates the street to gain   45
& steal into the fields of grain
From nights dull prison comes the duck
Waddling eager thro the muck
Squeezing thro the orchard pales
Where mornings bounty rarely fails   50
Eager gobbling as they pass
Dewworms thro the padded grass
Where blushing apples round & red
Load down the boughs & pat the head
Of longing maid that hither goes   55
To hang on lines the drying cloaths
Who views them oft with tempted eye
& steals one as she passes bye
    Where the holly oak so tall
Far oer tops the garden wall   60
That latest blooms for bees provide
Hived on stone benches close beside
The bees their teazing music hum
& threaten war to all that come
Save the old dame whose jealous care   65
Places a trapping bottle there
Filled with mock sweets in whose disguise
The honey loving hornet dies
    Upon the dovecoats mossy slates
The piegons coo around their mates   70
& beside the stable wall
Where morns sunbeams earliest fall
Basking hens in playfull rout
Flap the smoaking dust about
In the barn hole sits the cat   75

[February 1826]

Upon the dovecote's mossy slates, 35
The pigeons coo around their mates;
And close beside the stable wall,
Where morning sunbeams earliest fall,
The basking hen, in playful rout,
Flaps the powdery dust about. 40
Within the barn-hole sits the cat

1827

Watching within the thirsty rat
Who oft at morn its dwelling leaves
To drink the moisture from the eves
The redbreast with his nimble eye
Dare scarcely stop to catch the flye 80
That tangled in the spiders snare
Mourns in vain for freedom there
The dog beside the threshold lyes
Mocking sleep with half shut eyes
With head crouched down upon his feet 85
Till strangers pass his sunny seat
Then quick he pricks his ears to hark
& bustles up to growl & bark
While boys in fear stop short their song
& sneak on hurrys fears along 90
& beggar creeping like a snail
To make his hungry hopes prevail
Oer the warm heart of charity
Leaves his lame halt & hastens bye
  The maid afield now leaves the farm 95
With brimming bottles on her arm
Loitering unseen in narrow lane
To be oer took by following swain
Who happy thus her truth to prove
Carrys the load & talks of love 100
Full soon the harvest waggons sound
Rumbling like thunder all around
In ceasless speed the corn to load
Hurrying down the dusty road
While driving boy with eager eye 105
Watches the church clock passing bye
Whose gilt hands glitter in the sun
To see how far the hours have run
Right happly in the breathless day
To see it wearing fast away 110
Yet now & then a sudden shower
Will bring to toil a resting hour
When under sheltering shocks – a crowd
Of merry voices mingle loud
Wearing the shortlived boon along 115

[February 1826]

Watching to seize the thirsty rat,
Who oft at morn its dwelling leaves
To drink the moisture from the eaves;
The red-breast, with his nimble eye,   45
Dares scarcely stop to catch the fly,
That, tangled in the spider's snare,
Mourns in vain for freedom there.
The dog beside the threshold lies,
Mocking sleep, with half-shut eyes –   50
With head crouch'd down upon his feet,
Till strangers pass his sunny seat –
Then quick he pricks his ears to hark,
And bustles up to growl and bark;
While boys in fear stop short their song,   55
And sneak in startled speed along;
And beggar, creeping like a snail,
To make his hungry hopes prevail
O'er the warm heart of charity,
Leaves his lame halt and hastens by.   60
     The maid afield now leaves the farm,
With dinner basket on her arm,
Loitering unseen in narrow lane,
To be o'ertook by following swain,
Who, happy thus her truth to prove,   65
Carries the load and talks of love.
Soon as the dew is off the ground,
Rumbling like distant thunder round,
The waggons haste the corn to load,
And hurry down the dusty road;   70
While driving boy with eager eye
Watches the church clock passing by –
Whose gilt hands glitter in the sun –
To see how far the hours have run;
Right happy, in the breathless day,   75
To see time wearing fast away.
But now and then a sudden shower
Will bring to toil a resting hour;
Then, under sheltering shocks, a crowd
Of merry voices mingle loud,   80

1827

With vulgar tale & merry song
Draining with leisures laughing eye
Each welcome bubbling bottle drye
Till peeping suns dry up the rain
Then off they start to toil again   120
    Anon the fields are wearing clear
& glad sounds hum in labours ear
When childern halo "here they come"
& run to meet the harvest home
Stuck thick with boughs & thronged with boys   125
Who mingle loud a merry noise
Glad that the harvests end is nigh
& weary labour nearly bye
Where when they meet the stack thronged yard
Cross bunns or pence their shouts reward   130
    Then comes the harvest supper night
Which rustics welcome with delight
When merry game & tiresome tale
& songs increasing with the ale
Their mingled uproar interpose   135
To crown the harvests happy close
While rural mirth that there abides
Laughs till she almost cracks her sides
    Now harvests busy hum declines
& labour half its help resigns   140
Boys glad at heart to play return
The shepherds to their peace sojourn
Rush bosomed solitudes among
Which busy toil disturbed so long
The gossip happy all is oer   145
Visits again her neighbours door
For scandals idle tales to dwell
Which harvest had no time to tell
& free from all its sultry strife
Enjoy once more their idle life   150
Some that waining toil reprieves
Thread the forrests sea of leaves
Where the pheasant loves to hide
& the darkest glooms abide
Neath the old oaks mossed & grey   155

[February 1826]

Draining, with leisure's laughing eye,
Each welcome, bubbling bottle dry;
Till peeping suns dry up the rain,
Then off they start to toil again.
    Anon the fields are getting clear, 85
And glad sounds hum in labour's ear;
When children halloo "Here they come!"
And run to meet the Harvest Home,
Cover'd with boughs, and throng'd with boys,
Who mingle loud a merry noise, 90

And, when they meet the stack-throng'd yard,
Cross-buns and pence their shouts reward.
Then comes the harvest-supper night,
Which rustics welcome with delight;
When merry game and tiresome tale,
And songs, increasing with the ale, 95
Their mingled uproar interpose,
To crown the harvest's happy close;
While Mirth, that at the scene abides,
Laughs, till she almost cracks her sides.
    Now harvest's busy hum declines, 100
And labour half its help resigns.
Boys, glad at heart, to play return;
The shepherds to their peace sojourn,
Rush-bosom'd solitudes among, 105
Which busy toil disturb'd so long.
The gossip, happy all is o'er,
Visits again her neighbour's door,
On scandal's idle tales to dwell,
Which harvest had no time to tell; 110
And free from all its sultry strife,
Enjoys once more her idle life.
A few, whom waning toil reprieves,
Thread the forest's sea of leaves,
Where the pheasant loves to hide, 115
And the darkest glooms abide,
Beneath the old oaks moss'd and grey,

Whose shadows seem as old as they
Where time hath many seasons won
Since aught beneath them saw the sun
Within these bramble solitudes
The ragged noisey boy intrudes 160
To gather nuts that ripe & brown
As soon as shook will patter down
    Thus harvest ends its busy reign
& leaves the fields their peace again
Where autumns shadows idly muse 165
& tinge the trees with many hues
Amid whose scenes I'm feign to dwell
& sing of what I love so well
But hollow winds & tumbling floods
& humming showers & moaning woods 170
All startle into sudden strife
& wake a mighty lay to life
Making amid their strains divine
All songs in vain so mean as mine

[February 1826]

Whose shadows seem as old as they;
Where time hath many seasons won,
Since aught beneath them saw the sun; 120
Within these brambly solitudes,
The ragged, noisy boy intrudes,
To gather nuts, that, ripe and brown,
As soon as shook will patter down.
    Thus harvest ends its busy reign, 125
And leaves the fields their peace again;
Where Autumn's shadows idly muse
And tinge the trees in many hues:
Amid whose scenes I'm fain to dwell,
And sing of what I love so well. 130
But hollow winds, and tumbling floods,
And humming showers, and moaning woods,
All startle into sudden strife,
And wake a mighty lay to life;
Making, amid their strains divine, 135
Unheard a song so mean as mine.

1827

OCTOBER

OCTOBER[17]

[after autumn 1823 – March 1826]

Nature now spreads around in dreary hue
A pall to cover all that summer knew
Yet in the poets solitary way
Some pleasing objects for his praise delay
Somthing that makes him pause & turn again   5
As every trifle will his eye detain
The free horse rustling thro the stubble field
& cows at lare in rushes half conscealed
With groups of restless sheep who feed their fill
Oer cleard fields rambling were so ere they will   10
The geese flock gabbling in the splashy fields
& qua[c]king ducks in pondweeds half conseald
Or seeking worms along the homclose sward
Right glad of freedom from the prison yard
While every cart rut dribbles its low tide   15
& every hollow splashy sports provide
The hedger stopping gaps amid the leaves
That oer his head in every color weaves
The milk maid stepping with a timid look
From stone to stone across the brimming brook   20
The cotter journeying wi his noisey swine
Along the wood ride were the brambles twine
Shaking from dinted cups the acorns brown
& from the hedges red awes dashing down
While nutters rustling in the yellow woods   25
Still scare the wild things from their solitudes
& squirrels secret toils oer winter dreams
Picking the brown nuts from the yellow leams
& hunters from the thickets avenue
In scarlet jackets startling on the view   30
Skiming a moment oer the russet plain
Then hiding in the colord woods again
The ploping guns sharp momentary shock
Which eccho bustles from her cave to mock
The inly pleased tho solitary boy   35

October

1827

Nature now spreads around, in dreary hue,
A pall to cover all that summer knew;
Yet, in the poet's solitary way,
Some pleasing objects for his praise delay;
Something that makes him pause and turn again,   5
As every trifle will his eye detain: –
The free horse rustling through the stubble field;
And cows at lair in rushes, half conceal'd;
With groups of restless sheep who feed their fill,
O'er clear'd fields rambling wheresoe'er they will;   10

The hedger stopping gaps, amid the leaves,
Which time, o'er-head, in every colour weaves;
The milkmaid pausing with a timid look,
From stone to stone, across the brimming brook;
The cotter journeying with his noisy swine,   15
Along the wood-side where the brambles twine,
Shaking from mossy oaks the acorns brown,
Or from the hedges red haws dashing down;
The nutters, rustling in the yellow woods,
Who teaze the wild things in their solitudes;   20

The hunters, from the thicket's avenue,
In scarlet jackets, startling on the view,
Skimming a moment o'er the russet plain,
Then hiding in the motley woods again;
The plopping gun's sharp, momentary shock,   25
Which echo bustles from her cave to mock;
The bawling song of solitary boys,

Journeying & muttering oer his dreams of joy
Haunting the hedges for the wilding fruit
Of sloe or black berry just as fancys suit
The sticking groups in many a ragged set
Brushing the woods their harmless loads to get   40
& gipseys camps in some snug shelterd nook
Were old lane hedges like the pasture brook
Run crooking as they will by wood & dell
In such lone spots these wild wood roamers dwell
On commons were no farmers claims appear   45
Nor tyrant justice rides to interfere
Such the abodes neath hedge or spreading oak
& but discovered by its curling smoak
Puffing & peeping up as wills the breeze
Between the branches of the colord trees   50
Such are the pictures that october yields
To please the poet as he walks the fields
While nature like fair woman in decay
Which pale consumption hourly wastes away
Upon her waining features pale & chill   55
Wears dreams of beauty that seem lovely still
Among the heath furze still delights to dwell
Quaking as if with cold the harvest bell
The mushroom buttons each moist morning brings
Like spots of snow in the green tawney rings   60
& fuzz balls swelld like bladders in the grass
Which oft the merry laughing milking lass
Will stoop to gather in her sportive airs
& slive in mimickd fondness unawares
To smut the brown cheek of the teazing swain   65
With the black powder which their balls contain
Who feigns offence at first that love may speed
Then claims a kiss to recompence the deed
The singing maid in fancy ever gay
Loitering along the mornings dripping way   70
With wicker basket swinging on her arm
Searching the hedges of home close or farms[18]
Where brashy eldern trees to autumn fade
Wild shines each hedge in autumns gay parade
The glossy berrys picturesquely weaves   75

[after *autumn 1823 – March 1826*]

Journeying in rapture o'er their dreaming joys,
Haunting the hedges in their reveries,
For wilding fruit that shines upon the trees;   30

The wild wood music from the lonely dell,
Where merry Gipseys o'er their raptures dwell,
Haunting each common's wild and lonely nook,
Where hedges run as crooked as the brook,

Shielding their camps beneath some spreading oak, 35
And but discovered by the curling smoke
Puffing, and peeping up, as wills the breeze,
Between the branches of the coloured trees: –
Such are the pictures that October yields,
To please the poet as he walks the fields;   40
While Nature – like fair woman in decay,
Whom pale consumption hourly wastes away –
Upon her waning features, winter chill,
Wears dreams of beauty that seem lovely still.
Among the heath-furze still delights to dwell,   45
Quaking, as if with cold, the harvest bell;
And mushroom-buttons each moist morning brings,
Like spots of snow-shine in dark fairy rings.

Wild shines each hedge in autumn's gay parade;
And, where the eldern trees to autumn fade,   50
The glossy berry picturesquely cleaves

1827

Their swathy bunches mid the yellow leaves
Where the pert sparrow stains his little bill
& tutling robin picks his meals at will
Black ripening to the wan suns misty ray
Here the industr[i]ous hus wives wend their way   80
Pulling the brittle branches carefull down
& hawking loads of berrys to the town
While village dames as they get ripe & fine
Repair to pluck them for their "eldern wine"
That bottld up becomes a rousing charm   85
To kindle winters icy bosom warm
That wi its merry partner nut brown beer
Makes up the peasants christmass keeping cheer

The flying clouds urged on in swiftest pace
Like living things as if they runned a race   90
The winds that oer each coming tempest broods
Waking like spirits in their startling moods
Fluttering the sear leaves on the blackning lea
That litters under every fading tree
& pausing oft as falls the patting rain   95
Then gathering strength & twirling them again

The startld stockdove hurried wizzing bye
As the still hawk hangs oer him in the sky
Crows from the oak trees quawking as they spring
Dashing the acorns down wi beating wing   100
Waking the woodlands sleep in noises low
Patting the crimpt brakes withering brown below
The starnel crowds that dim the muddy light
& puddock circling round its lazy flight
Round the wild sweeing wood in motion slow   105
Before it perches on the oaks below
& hugh black beetles revelling alone
In the dull evening with their heavy drone
Buzzing from barn door straw & hovel sides
Were fodderd cattle from the night abides   110

[after *autumn 1823 – March 1826*]

Its swarthy bunches 'mid the yellow leaves,
On which the tootling robin feeds at will,
And coy hedge-sparrow stains its little bill.

The village dames, as they get ripe and fine,   55
Gather the bunches for their "eldern wine;"
Which, bottled up, becomes a rousing charm,
To kindle winter's icy bosom warm;
And, with its merry partner, nut-brown beer,
Makes up the peasant's Christmas-keeping cheer.   60

   Like to a painted map the landscape lies;[19]
And wild above, shine the cloud-thronged skies,
That chase each other on with hurried pace,
Like living things, as if they ran a race.
The winds, that o'er each sudden tempest brood,   65
Waken like spirits in a startled mood;
Flirting the sear leaves on the bleaching lea,
That litter under every fading tree;
And pausing oft, as falls the patting rain;
Then gathering strength, and twirling them again,   70
Till drops the sudden calm: – the hurried mill[20]
Is stopt at once, and every noise is still;

Save crows, that from the oak trees quawking spring,
Dashing the acorns down with beating wing,
Waking the wood's short sleep in noises low,   75
Patting the crimpt brakes withering brown below;
And whirr of starling crowds, that dim the light
With mimic darkness, in their numerous flight;
Or shrilly noise of puddocks' feeble wail,
As in slow circles round the woods they sail;   80
While huge black beetles, revelling alone,
In the dull evening hum their heavy drone.

1827

These pictures linger thro the shortning day
& cheer the lone bards mellancholy way

[after *autumn 1823 – March 1826]*

These trifles linger through the shortening day,
To cheer the lone bard's solitary way;
Till surly Winter comes with biting breath,[21]   85
And strips the woods, and numbs the scene with death;
Then all is still o'er wood and field and plain,
As nought had been, and nought would be again.

1827

NOVEMBER

NOVEMBER²²

[February/April 1824 – February/March 1826]

The village sleeps in mist from morn till noon
& if the sun wades thro tis wi a face
Beamless & pale & round as if the moon
When done the journey of its nightly race
Had found him sleeping & supplyd his place   5
For days the shepherds in the fields may be
Nor mark a patch of sky – blind fold they trace
The plains that seem wi out a bush or tree
Wistling aloud by guess to flocks they cannot see

The timid hare seems half its fears to loose   10
Crouching & sleeping neath its grassy lare
& scarcly startles tho the shepherd goes
Close by its home & dogs are barking there
The wild colt only turns around to stare
At passers bye then naps his hide again   15
& moody crows beside the road forbeer
To flye tho pelted by the passing swain
Thus day seems turned to night & trys to wake in vain

The Owlet leaves her hiding place at noon
& flaps her grey wings in the doubting light   20
The hoarse jay screams to see her out so soon
& small birds chirp & startle with affright
Much doth it scare the superstitious wight
Who dreams of sorry luck & sore dismay
While cow boys think the day a dream of night   25
& oft grow fearful on their lonely way
Who fancy ghosts may wake & leave their graves by day

The cleanly maiden thro the village streets
In pattens clicks down causways never drye
While eves above head drops – were oft she meets   30
The school boy leering on wi mischiefs eye
Trying to splash her as he hurrys bye

November

1827

The landscape sleeps in mist from morn till noon;
    And, if the sun looks through, 'tis with a face
    Beamless and pale and round, as if the moon,
    When done the journey of her nightly race,
    Had found him sleeping, and supplied his place.   5
    For days the shepherds in the fields may be,
    Nor mark a patch of sky – blindfold they trace,
    The plains, that seem without a bush or tree,
Whistling aloud by guess, to flocks they cannot see.

The timid hare seems half its fears to lose,   10
    Crouching and sleeping 'neath its grassy lair,
    And scarcely startles, tho' the shepherd goes
    Close by its home, and dogs are barking there;
    The wild colt only turns around to stare
    At passer by, then knaps his hide again;   15
    And moody crows beside the road, forbear
    To fly, tho' pelted by the passing swain;
Thus day seems turn'd to night, and tries to wake in vain.

The owlet leaves her hiding-place at noon,
    And flaps her grey wings in the doubling light;   20
    The hoarse jay screams to see her out so soon,
    And small birds chirp and startle with affright;
    Much doth it scare the superstitious wight,
    Who dreams of sorry luck, and sore dismay;
    While cow-boys think the day a dream of night,   25
    And oft grow fearful on their lonely way,
Fancying that ghosts may wake, and leave their graves by day.

While swains afield returning to their ploughs
Their passing aid wi gentle speech apply
& much loves rapture thrills when she alows
Their help wi offerd hand to lead her oer the sloughs   35

The hedger soakd wi the dull weather chops
On at his toils which scarcly keeps him warm
& every stroke he takes large swarms of drops
Patter about him like an april storm
The sticking dame wi cloak upon her arm   40
To guard against a storm walks the wet leas
Of willow groves or hedges round the farm
Picking up aught her splashy wanderings sees
Dead sticks the sudden winds have shook from off the trees 45

The boy that scareth from the spirey wheat
The mellancholy crow – quakes while he weaves
Beneath the ivey tree a hut & seat
Of rustling flags & sedges tyd in sheaves
Or from nigh stubble shocks a shelter thieves   50
There he doth dithering sit or entertain
His leisure hours down hedges lost to leaves
While spying nests where he spring eggs hath taen
He wishes in his heart twas summer time again

& oft he ll clamber up a sweeing tree   55
To see the scarlet hunter hurry bye
& feign woud in their merry uproar be
But sullen labour hath its tethering tye
Crows swop around & some on bushes nigh
Watch for a chance when ere he turns away   60
To settle down their hunger to supply
From morn to eve his toil demands his stay
Save now & then an hour which leisure steals for play

Gaunt grey hounds now their coursing sports impart
Wi long legs stretchd on tip toe for the chase   65
& short loose ear & eye upon the start
Swift as the wind their motio[n]s they unlace
When bobs the hare up from her hiding place

[February/April 1824 – February/March 1826]

Who in its furry coat of fallow stain
Squats on the lands or wi a dodging pace   70
Tryes its old coverts of wood grass to gain
& oft by cunning ways makes all their speed in vain

Dull for a time the slumbering weather flings
Its murky prison round then winds wake loud
Wi sudden start the once still forest sings   75
Winters returning song cloud races cloud
& the orison throws away its shrowd
& sweeps its stretching circle from the eye
Storm upon storm in quick succession crowd
& oer the samness of the purple skye   80
Heaven paints its wild irregularity

The shepherd oft foretells by simple ways
The weathers change that will ere long prevail
He marks the dull ass that grows wild & brays
& sees the old cows gad adown the vale   85
A summer race & snuff the coming gale
The old dame sees her cat wi fears alarm
Play hurly burly races wi its tale
& while she stops her wheel her hands to warm
She rubs her shooting corns & prophecys a storm   90

Morts are the signs – the stone hid toad will croak
& gobbling turkey cock wi noises vile
Dropping his snout as flaming as a cloak
Loose as a red rag oer his beak the while
Urging the dame to turn her round & smile   95
To see his uncooth pride her cloaths attack
Sidling wi wings hung down in vapourey broil
& feathers ruffld up while oer his back
His tail spreads like a fan cross wavd wi bars of black

The hog sturts round the stye & champs the straw   100
& bolts about as if a dog was bye
The steer will cease its gulping cud to chew
& toss his head wi wild & startld eye
At windshook straws – the geese will noise & flye

[February/April 1824 – February/March 1826]

Yet but awhile the slumbering weather flings
    Its murky prison round – then winds wake loud;
    With sudden stir the startled forest sings   30
    Winter's returning song – cloud races cloud,
    And the horizon throws away its shroud,
    Sweeping a stretching circle from the eye;
    Storms upon storms in quick succession crowd,
    And o'er the sameness of the purple sky   35
Heaven paints, with hurried hand, wild hues of every dye.

1827

Like wild ones to the pond – wi matted mane   105
The cart horse squeals & kicks his partner nigh
While leaning oer his fork the foddering swain
The uproar marks around & dreams of wind & rain

& quick it comes among the forest oaks
Wi sobbing ebbs & uproar gathering high   110
The scard hoarse raven on its cradle croaks
& stock dove flocks in startld terrors flye
While the blue hawk hangs oer them in the skye
The shepherd happy when the day is done
Hastes to his evening fire his cloaths to dry   115
& forrester crouchd down the storm to shun
Scarce hears amid the strife the poachers muttering gun

The ploughman hears the sudden storm begin
& hies for shelter from his naked toil
Buttoning his doublet closer to his chin   120
He speeds him hasty oer the elting soil
While clouds above him in wild fury boil
& winds drive heavily the beating rain
He turns his back to catch his breath awhile
Then ekes his speed & faces it again   125
To seek the shepherds hut beside the rushy plain

Oft stripping cottages & barns of thack
Were startld farmer garnerd up his grain
& wheat & bean & oat & barley stack
Leaving them open to the beating rain   130
The husbandman grieves oer his loss in vain
& sparrows mourn their night nests spoild & bare
The thackers they resume their toils again
& stubbornly the tall red ladders bare
While to oerweight the wind they hang old harrows there   135

Thus wears the month along in checkerd moods
Sunshine & shadow tempests loud & calms
One hour dyes silent oer the sleepy woods
The next wakes loud with unexpected storms
A dreary nakedness the field deforms   140

[February/April 1824 – February/March 1826]

At length it comes among the forest oaks,
    With sobbing ebbs, and uproar gathering high;
    The scared, hoarse raven on its cradle croaks,
    And stockdove-flocks in hurried terrors fly,   40
    While the blue hawk hangs o'er them in the sky. –
    The hedger hastens from the storm begun,
    To seek a shelter that may keep him dry;
    And foresters low bent, the wind to shun,
Scarce hear amid the strife the poacher's muttering gun.   45

The ploughman hears its humming rage begin,
    And hies for shelter from his naked toil;
    Buttoning his doublet closer to his chin,
    He bends and scampers o'er the elting soil,
    While clouds above him in wild fury boil,   50
    And winds drive heavily the beating rain;
    He turns his back to catch his breath awhile,
    Then ekes his speed and faces it again,
To seek the shepherd's hut beside the rushy plain.

The boy, that scareth from the spiry wheat   55
    The melancholy crow – in hurry weaves,
    Beneath an ivied tree, his sheltering seat,
    Of rushy flags and sedges tied in sheaves,
    Or from the field a shock of stubble thieves.
    There he doth dithering sit, and entertain   60
    His eyes with marking the storm-driven leaves;
    Oft spying nests where he spring eggs had ta'en,
And wishing in his heart 'twas summer time again.

Thus wears the month along, in checker'd moods,
    Sunshine and shadows, tempests loud, and calms;   65
    One hour dies silent o'er the sleepy woods,
    The next wakes loud with unexpected storms;
    A dreary nakedness the field deforms –

1827

Yet many rural sounds & rural sights
Live in the village still about the farms
Where toils rude uproar hums from morn till night
Noises in which the ear of industry delights

Hoarse noise of field-free bull that strides ahead   145
Of the tail switching herd to feed again
The barking mastiff from his kennel bed
Urging his teazing noise at passing swain
The jostling rumble of the sturting wain
From the farm yard were freedoms chance to wait   150
The turkey drops his snout – & geese in vain
Noise at the signal of the opening gate
Then from the clowns whip flyes & finds the chance too late

The pigeon wi its breast of many hues
That spangles to the sun turns round & round   155
About his timid sidling mate & croos
Upon the cottage ridge were oer their heads
The puddock sails oft swopping oer the pen
Were timid chickens from their parent stray
That skulk & scutter neath her wings agen   160
Nor peeps no more till they have saild away
& one bye one they peep & hardly dare to stray[23]

Such rural sounds the mornings tongue renews
& rural sights swarm on the rustics eye
The billy goat shakes from his beard the dews   165
& jumps the wall wi carting teams to hie
Upon the barn rig at their freedom flye
The spotted guiney fowl – hogs in the stye
Agen the door in rooting whinings stand
The freed colt drops his head & gallops bye   170
The boy that holds a scuttle in his hand
Prefering unto toil the commons rushy land[24]

At length the noise of busy toil is still
& industry awhile her care forgoes
When winter comes in earnest to fulfil   175
Her yearly task at bleak novembers close

[February/April 1824 – February/March 1826]

Yet many a rural sound, and rural sight,
  Lives in the village still about the farms, 70
    Where toil's rude uproar hums from morn till night
Noises, in which the ear of Industry delights.

At length the stir of rural labour's still,
  And Industry awhile her care foregoes;
    When Winter comes in earnest to fulfil 75
  His yearly task, at bleak November's close,

1827

& stops the plough & hides the field in snows
When frost locks up the streams in chill delay
& mellows on the hedge the purple sloes
For little birds – then toil hath time for play   180
& nought but threshers flails awake the dreary day

[February/April 1824 – February/March 1826]

And stops the plough, and hides the field in snows;
When frost locks up the stream in chill delay,
And mellows on the hedge the jetty sloes,
For little birds – then Toil hath time for play,   80
And nought but threshers' flails awake the dreary day.

December

December
Christmass

[autumn 1823 – March 1826]

Christmass is come & every hearth
Makes room to give him welcome now
Een want will dry its tears in mirth
& crown him wi a holly bough
Tho tramping neath a winter sky   5
Oer snow track paths & ryhmey stiles
The hus wife sets her spinning bye
& bids him welcome wi her smiles

Each house is swept the day before
& windows stuck wi evergreens   10
The snow is beesomd from the door
& comfort crowns the cottage scenes
Gilt holly wi its thorny pricks
& yew & box wi berrys small
These deck the unusd candlesticks   15
& pictures hanging by the wall

Neighbours resume their anual cheer
Wishing wi smiles & spirits high
Glad christmass & a happy year
To every morning passer bye   20
Milk maids their christmass journeys go
Accompanyd wi favourd swain
& childern pace the crumping snow
To taste their grannys cake again

Hung wi the ivys veining bough   25
The ash trees round the cottage farm
Are often stript of branches now
The cotters christmass hearth to warm
He swings & twists his hazel band
& lops them off wi sharpend hook   30
& oft brings ivy in his hand
To decorate the chimney nook

December

1827

GLAD Christmas comes, and every hearth
   Makes room to give him welcome now,
E'en want will dry its tears in mirth,
   And crown him with a holly bough;
Though tramping 'neath a winter sky,   5
   O'er snowy paths and rimy stiles,
The housewife sets her spinning by
   To bid him welcome with her smiles.

Each house is swept the day before,
   And windows stuck with ever-greens,   10
The snow is besom'd from the door,
   And comfort crowns the cottage scenes.
Gilt holly, with its thorny pricks,
   And yew and box, with berries small,
These deck the unused candlesticks,   15
   And pictures hanging by the wall.

Neighbours resume their annual cheer,
   Wishing, with smiles and spirits high,
Glad Christmas and a happy year,
   To every morning passer-by;   20
Milkmaids their Christmas journeys go,
   Accompanied with favour'd swain;
And children pace the crumping snow,
   To taste their granny's cake again.

Old winter whipes his icles bye
& warms his fingers till he smiles
Were cottage hearths are blazing high   35
& labour resteth from his toils
Wi merry mirth beguiling care
Old customs keeping wi the day
Friends meet their christmass cheer to share
& pass it in a harmless way   40

Old customs O I love the sound
However simple they may be
What ere wi time has sanction found
Is welcome & is dear to me
Pride grows above simplicity   45
& spurns it from her haughty mind
& soon the poets song will be
The only refuge they can find

The shepherd now no more afraid
Since custom doth the chance bestow   50
Starts up to kiss the giggling maid
Beneath the branch of mizzletoe
That neath each cottage beam is seen
Wi pearl-like-berrys shining gay
The shadow still of what hath been   55
Which fashion yearly fades away

& singers too a merry throng
A[t] early morn wi simple skill
Yet imitate the angels song
& chant their christmass ditty still   60
& mid the storm that dies & swells
By fits – in humings softly steals
The music of the village bells
Ringing round their merry peals

& when its past a merry crew   65
Bedeckt in masks & ribbons gay
The "Morrice dance" their sports renew
& act their winter evening play

[autumn 1823 – March 1826]

The shepherd, now no more afraid,   25
   Since custom doth the chance bestow,
Starts up to kiss the giggling maid
   Beneath the branch of misletoe
That 'neath each cottage beam is seen,
   With pearl-like berries shining gay;   30
The shadow still of what hath been,
   Which fashion yearly fades away.

The singing wates, a merry throng,
   At early morn, with simple skill,
Yet imitate the angels song,   35
   And chant their Christmas ditty still;
And, 'mid the storm that dies and swells
   By fits – in hummings softly steals
The music of the village bells,
   Ringing round their merry peals.   40

When this is past, a merry crew,
   Bedeck'd in masks and ribbons gay,
The "Morris-dance," their sports renew,
   And act their winter evening play.

1827

The clown-turnd-kings for penny praise
Storm wi the actors strut & swell 70
& harlequin a laugh to raise
Wears his hump back & tinkling bell

& oft for pence & spicy ale
Wi winter nosgays pind before
The wassail singer tells her tale 75
& drawls her christmass carrols oer
The prentic[e] boy wi ruddy face
& ryhme bepowdered dancing locks
From door to door wi happy pace
Runs round to claim his "christmass box" 80

The block behind the fire is put
To sanction customs old desires
& many a faggots bands are cut
For the old farmers christmass fires
Were loud tongd gladness joins the throng 85
& winter meets the warmth of may
Feeling by times the heat too strong
& rubs his shins & draws away

While snows the window panes bedim
The fire curls up a sunny charm 90
Were creaming oer the pitchers rim
The flowering ale is set to warm
Mirth full of joy as summer bees
Sits there its pleasures to impart
While children tween their parents knees 95
Sing scraps of carrols oer by heart

& some to view the winter weathers
Climb up the window seat wi glee
Likening the snow to falling feathers
In fancys infant extacy 100
Laughing wi superstitions love
Oer visions wild that youth supplyes
Of people pulling geese above
& keeping christmass in the skyes

[autumn 1823 – March 1826]

The clown turn'd king, for penny-praise,   45
    Storms with the actor's strut and swell;
And Harlequin, a laugh to raise,
    Wears his hunch-back and tinkling bell.

And oft for pence and spicy ale,
    With winter nosegays pinn'd before,   50
The wassail-singer tells her tale,
    And drawls her Christmas carols o'er.
While 'prentice boy, with ruddy face,
    And rime-bepowder'd, dancing locks,
From door to door with happy pace,   55
    Runs round to claim his "Christmas box."

The block upon the fire is put,
    To sanction custom's old desires;
And many a fagot's bands are cut,
    For the old farmers' Christmas fires;   60
Where loud-tongued Gladness joins the throng,
    And Winter meets the warmth of May,
Till feeling soon the heat too strong,
    He rubs his shins, and draws away.

While snows the window-panes bedim,   65
    The fire curls up a sunny charm,
Where, creaming o'er the pitcher's rim,
    The flowering ale is set to warm;
Mirth, full of joy as summer bees,
    Sits there, its pleasures to impart,   70
And children, 'tween their parent's knees,
    Sing scraps of carols o'er by heart.

And some, to view the winter weathers,
    Climb up the window-seat with glee,
Likening the snow to falling feathers,   75
    In Fancy's infant ecstasy;
Laughing, with superstitious love,
    O'er visions wild that youth supplies,
Of people pulling geese above,
    And keeping Christmas in the skies.   80

1827

As tho the homstead trees were drest   105
In lieu of snow wi dancing leaves
As tho the sun dryd martins nest
Instead of icles hung the eaves
The childern hail the happy day
As if the snow was april grass   110
& pleasd as neath the warmth of may
Sport oer the water froze to glass

Tho[u] day of happy sound & mirth
That long wi childish memory stays
How blest around the cottage hearth   115
I met thee in my boyish days
Harping wi raptures dreaming joys
Oer presents that thy coming found
The welcome sight of little toys
The christmass gifts of commers round   120

The wooden horse wi arching head
Drawn upon wheels around the room
The gilded coach of ginger bread
& many colord sugar plumb
Gilt coverd books for pictures sought   125
Or storys childhood loves to tell
Wi many a urgent promise bought
To get tomorrows lesson well

& many a thing a minutes sport
Left broken on the sanded floor   130
When we woud leave our play & court
Our parents promises for more
Tho manhood bids such raptures dye
& throws such toys away as vain
Yet memory loves to turn her eye   135
& talk such pleasures oer again

Around the glowing hearth at night
The harmless laugh & winter tale
Goes round – while parting friends delight
To toast each other oer their ale   140

[autumn 1823 – March 1826]

As tho' the homestead trees were drest,
    In lieu of snow, with dancing leaves;
As tho' the sun-dried martin's nest,
    Instead of i'cles hung the eaves;
The children hail the happy day –   85
    As if the snow were April's grass,
And pleas'd, as 'neath the warmth of May,
    Sport o'er the water froze to glass.

Thou day of happy sound and mirth,
    That long with childish memory stays,   90
How blest around the cottage hearth
    I met thee in my younger days!
Harping, with rapture's dreaming joys,
    On presents which thy coming found,
The welcome sight of little toys,   95
    The Christmas gift of cousins round.

The wooden horse with arching head,
    Drawn upon wheels around the room;
The gilded coach of gingerbread,
    And many-colour'd sugar plum;   100
Gilt cover'd books for pictures sought,
    Or stories childhood loves to tell,
With many an urgent promise bought,
    To get to-morrow's lesson well.

And many a thing, a minute's sport,   105
    Left broken on the sanded floor,
When we would leave our play, and court
    Our parents' promises for more.
Tho' manhood bids such raptures die,
    And throws such toys aside as vain,   110
Yet memory loves to turn her eye,
    And count past pleasures o'er again.

Around the glowing hearth at night,
    The harmless laugh and winter tale
Go round, while parting friends delight   115
    To toast each other o'er their ale;

1827

The cotter oft wi quiet zeal
Will musing oer his bible lean
While in the dark the lovers steal
To kiss & toy behind the screen

The yule cake dotted thick wi plumbs　　　145
Is on each supper table found
& cats look up for falling crumbs
Which greedy childern litter round
& hus wifes sage stuffd seasond chine
Long hung in chimney nook to drye　　　150
& boiling eldern berry wine
To drink the christmass eves "good bye"

[autumn 1823 – March 1826]

The cotter oft with quiet zeal
   Will musing o'er his Bible lean;
While in the dark the lovers steal
   To kiss and toy behind the screen.   120

Old customs! Oh! I love the sound,
   However simple they may be:
Whate'er with time hath sanction found,
   Is welcome, and is dear to me.
Pride grows above simplicity,   125
   And spurns them from her haughty mind,
And soon the poet's song will be
   The only refuge they can find.

1827

Appendix A

The First Version of 'July'

The debate about the imaginative quality and length of Clare's first version of 'July' is discussed in the introduction (p. xviii above). So that readers can assess the justice or injustice of Taylor's criticisms, the complete first version of the month is presented here. The revised, 'final' version is presented against the 1827 text on pp. 124–33 above.

Daughter of pastoral smells & sights
& sultry days & dewy nights
July resumes her yearly place
Wi her milking maiden face
Ruddy & tannd yet sweet to view   5
When everyweres a veil of dew
& raps it round her looks that smiles
A lovly rest to daily toils
Wi last months closing scenes & dins
Her sultry beaming birth begins   10
Hay makers still in grounds appear
& some are thinning nearly clear
Save oddling lingering shocks about
Which the tithman counteth out
Sticking their green boughs were they go   15
The parsons yearly claims to know
Which farmers view wi grudging eye
& grumbling drive their waggons bye
In hedge bound close & meadow plains
Stript groups of busy bustling swains   20
From all her hants wi noises rude
Drives to the wood lands solitude
That seeks a spot unmarkd wi paths
Far from the close & meadow swaths
Wi smutty song & story gay   25
They cart the witherd smelling hay

Boys loading on the waggon stand
& men below wi sturdy hand
Heave up the shocks on lathy prong
While horse boys lead the team along   30
& maidens drag the rake behind
Wi light dress shaping to the wind
& trembling locks of curly hair
& snow white bosoms nearly bare
That charms ones sight amid the hay   35
Like lingering blossoms of the may
From clowns rude jokes the[y] often turn
& oft their cheeks wi blushes burn
From talk which to escape a sneer
They oft affect as not to hear   40
Some in the nooks about the ground
Pile up the stacks swelld bellying round
The milking cattles winter fare
That in the snow are fodderd there
Warm spots wi black thorn thickets lind   45
& trees to brake the no[r]thern wind
While masters oft the sultry hours
Will urge their speed & talk of showers
When boy from home trotts to the stack
Wi dinner upon dobbins back   50
& bottles to the saddle tyd
Or ballancd upon either side
A horse thats past his toiling day
Yet still a favorite in his way
That trotts on errands up & down   55
The fields & too & fro from town
Long ere his presence comes in sight
Boys listen wi heart felt delight
& know his footsteps down the road
Hastening wi the dinner load   60
Then they seek in close or meadows
High hedgerows wi grey willow shadows
To hide beneath from sultry noon
& rest them at their dinner boon
Were helping shepherd for the lass   65
Will seek a hillock on the grass

The thickset hedge or stack beside
Were teazing pismires near abide
& when tis found down drops the maid
Proud wi the kind attention paid 70
& still the swain wi notice due
Waits on her all the dinner through
& fills her horn which she tho dry
In shoyness often pushes bye
While he will urge wi many a smile 75
It as a strength to help her toil
& in her hand will oft contrive
From out his pocket pulld to slive
Stole fruit when no one turns his eye
To wet her mouth when shes adry 80
Offerd when she refuses ale
Noons sultry labour to regale
Teazd wi the countless multitude
Of flyes that every were intrude
While boys wi boughs will often try 85
To beat them from them as they lye
Who find their labour all in vain
& soon as ceasd they swarm again
Thus while each swain & boy & lass
Sit at their dinner on the grass 90
The teams wi gears thrown on their backs
Stand pulling at the shocks or racks
Switching their tails & turning round
To knap the gadflys teazing wound
While dob that brought the dinners load 95
Too tricky to be turnd abroad
Needing the scuttle shook wi grain
To coax him to be caught again
Is to a tree at tether tyd
Ready for boy to mount & ride 100
Nipping the grass about his pound
& stamping battering hooves around
Soon as each ground is clear of hay
The shepherd whoops his flocks away
From follow fields¹ to plentys scen[e]s 105
Shining as smooth as bowling greens

But scard wi clipping tides alarms
They bleat about the close in swarms
& hide neath hedges in the cool
Still panting tho wi out their whool   110
Markd wi the tard brands lasting dye
& make a restless hue & cry
Answering the lambs that call again
& for their old dams seek in vain
Running mid the stranger throng   115
& ever meeting wi the wrong
Fiegn wi some old yoe to abide
Who smells & tosses them aside
& some as if they knew its face
Will meet a lamb wi mended pace   120
But proving hopes indulgd in vain
They turn around & blair again
Till weand from memory half forgot
They spread & feed & notice not
Save now & then to lambs shrill crys   125
Odd yoes in hoarser tone replys
Still may be seen the mowing swain
On balks between the fields of grain
Who often stops his thirst to ease
To pick the juicy pods of pease   130
& oft as chances bring to pass
Stoops oer his scyth stick in the grass
To suck the brimming honey comb
Which bees so long were toiling home
& rifld from so many flowers   135
& carried thro so many hours
He tears their small hives mossy ball
Were the brown labourers hurded all
Who gather homward one by one
& see their nest & honey gone   140
Humming around his rushy toil
Their melancholly wrongs awhile
Then oer the sweltering swaths they stray
& hum disconsolate away
& oft neath hedges cooler screen   145
Were meadow sorrel lingers green

Calld "sour grass" by the knowing clown
The mower gladly chews it down
& slakes his thirst the best he may
When singing brooks are far away   150
& his hoopd bottle woeful tale
Is emptied of its cheering ale
That lulld him in unconscous sleep
At dinners hour beneath a heap
Of grass or bush or edding shock   155
Till startld by the country clock
That told the hour[s] his toil had lost
Who coud but spare an hour at most
& wearing past the setting sun
He stays to get his labour done   160
The gipsey down the meadow brook
Wi long pole & [a] reaping hook
Tyd at its end amid the streams
That glitters wi the hot sunbeams
Reaches & cuts the bulrush down   165
& hawks them round each neighboring town
Packd at his back or tyd in loads
On asses down the dusty roads
He jogs & shouts from door to door
His well known note of calling oer   170
Offering to hus wives cheap repairs
Mending their broken bottomd chairs
Wi step half walk half dance & eye
Ready to smile on passers bye
Wi load well suiting weather warm   175
Tuckd carlessly beneath his arm
Or peeping coat & side between
In woolen bag of faded green
Half conseald & half displayd
A purpose tell tale to his trade   180
The gipsey fiddler jogs away
To village feast & holiday
Scraping in public house to trye
What beer his music will supply
From clowns who happy wi the din   185
Dance their hard naild hilos thin

Along the roads in passing crowds
Followd by dust like smoaking clouds
Scotch droves of beast a little breed
In swelterd weary mood proceed   190
A patient race from scottish hills
To fatten by our pasture rills
Lean wi the wants of mountain soil
But short & stout for travels toil
Wi cockd up horns & curly crown   195
& dewlap bosom hanging down
Followd by slowly pacing swains
Wild to our rushy flats & plains
At whom the shepherds dog will rise
& shake himself & in supprise   200
Draws back & waffles in affright
Barking the traveller out of sight
& mowers oer their scythes will bear
Upon their uncouth dress to stare
& shepherds as they trample bye   205
Leaves oer their hooks a wondering eye
To witness men so oddly clad
In petticoats of banded plad
Wi blankets oer their shoulders slung
To camp at night the fields among   210
When they for rest on commons stop
& blue cap like a stocking top
Cockt oer their faces summer brown
Wi scarlet tazzeles on the crown
Rude patterns of the thistle flower   215
Unbrinkd & open to the shower
& honest faces frank & free
That breath of mountain liberty
Soon as the morning wakens red
The shepherd startles from his bed   220
& rocks afield his morning pace
While folded sheep will know his face
Rising as he appears in sight
To shake their coats as in delight
His shadow stalking stride for stride   225
Stretches a jiant by his side

Long as a tree without a top
& oft it urges him to stop
Both in his journey & his song
& wonders why it seems so long   230
& bye & bye as morning dies
Shrinks to a unbrichd boy in size
Then as the evening gathers blue
Grows to a jiants length anew
Puzzld the more he stops to pause   235
His wisdom vainly seeks the cause
Again his journey he pursues
Lengthening his track along the dews
& his dog that turnd to pick
From his sides the sucking tick   240
Insects that on cattle creep
& bites the labourer laid asleep
Pricks up his ears to see him gone
& shakes his hide & hastens on
& the while the shepherd stayd   245
Trailing a track the hare had made
Bolts thro the creeping hedge again
& hurring follows wi the swain
The singing shouting herding boys
Follows again their wild employs   250
& ere the sun puts half his head
From out his crimson pillowd bed
& bawls behind his cows again
That one by one lobs down the lane
Wi wild weeds in his hat anew   255
The summer sorts of every hue
& twigs of leaves that please his eye
To his old haunts he hallows bye
Wi dog that loiters by his side
Or trotts before wi nimble stride   260
That waits till bid to bark & run
& panteth from the dreaded sun
& oft amid the sunny day
Will join a partner in his play
& in his antic tricks & glee   265
Will prove as fond of sport as he

& by the flag pool summer warm
He ll watch the motions of his arm
That holds a stick or stone to throw
In the sun gilded flood below   270
& head oer ears he da[n]ses in
Nor fears to wet his curly skin
The boys peeld cudgel to restore
& brings it in his mouth ashore
& eager as for crust or bone   275
He ll run to catch the pelted stone
Till wearied out he shakes his hide
& drops his tail & sneaks aside
Unheeding whistles shouts & calls
To take a rest were thickly falls   280
The rush clumps shadows there he lyes
Licking his skin & catching flyes
Or picking tween his stretching feet
The bone he had not time to eat
Before when wi the teazing boy   285
He was so throngd wi plays employ
Noon gathers wi its blistering breath
Around & day dyes still as death
The breeze is stopt the lazy bough
Hath not a leaf that dances now   290
The totter grass upon the hill
& spiders threads is hanging still
The feathers dropt from morehens wings
Upon the waters surface clings
As stedfast & as heavy seem   295
As stones beneath them in the stream
Hawkweed & groundsels fairey downs
Unruffld keep their seeding crowns
& in the oven heated air
Not one light thing is floating there   300
Save that to the earnest eye
The restless heat swims twittering bye
The swine run restless down the street
Anxious some pond or ditch to meet
From days hot swoonings to retire   305
Wallowing in the weeds & mire

The linnets seek the twiggs that lye
Close to the brook & brig stones drye
At top & sit & dip their bills
Till they have drunk their little fills   310
Then flert their wings & wet their feathers
To cool them in the blazing weathers
Dashing the water oer their heads
Then high them to some cooling sheds
Some dark wood glooms about the plain   315
To pick their feathers smooth again
The young qui[c]ks branches seem as dead
& scorch from yellow into red
Ere autum hath its pencil taen
Their shades in different hues to stain   320
Following behind the cranking ploughs
Whiping oft their sweating brows
The boys lead horses yokd in pairs
To jumping harrows linkd that tears
& teazes the hard clods to dust   325
Placing for showers in hopes their trust
The farmer follows sprinkling round
Wi turnip seed the panting ground
Providing food for beast & sheep
When winters snows are falling deep   330
Oft proving hopes & wishes vain
While clouds disperse that promisd rain
While soon as ere the turnip creeps
From out the crust burnt soil & peeps
Upon the farmers watching eye   335
Tis eaten by the jumping flye
& eager neath the midday sun
Soon as each plough teams toil is done
Scarse waiting till the gears are taen
From off their backs by boy & swain   340
From hay filld racks they turn away
Nor in the stable care to stay
Hurring to the trough to drink
Or from the yard ponds muddy brink
Rush in & wi long winded soak   345
Drink till theyre almost fit to choak

& from the horsbees teazing din
Thrust deep their burning noses in
Almost above their greedy eyes
To cool their mouths & shun the flyes   350
Deaf to the noise the geese will make
That grudge the worthy share they take
Boys now neath green lanes meeting bough
Each noons half holiday from plough
Take out their hungry teams till night   355
That nipp the grass wi eager bite
Wi long tails switching never still
They lunge neath trees when eat their fill
& stamp & switch till closing day
Brushing the teazing flyes away   360
Endless labour all in vain
That start in crowds to turn again
When the sun is sinking down
& dyes more deep the shadows brown
& gradual into slumber glooms   365
How sweet the village evening comes
To weary hinds from toil releasd
& panting sheep & torturd beast
The shepherd long wi heat opprest
Betakes him to his cottage rest   370
& his tird dog that plods along
Wi panting breath & lolling tongue
Runs eager as the brook appears
& dashes in head over ears
Startling reed sparrow broods to flye   375
That in the reed woods slumberd nigh
& water voles in haste to hide
Nibbling the sedges close beside
Lapping while he floats about
To quench his thirst then drabbles out   380
& shakes his coat & like the swain
Is happy night is come again
The beast that to the pond did creep
& rushd in water belly deep
The gad flyes threatning hums to shun   385
& horse bee darting in the sun

Lashing their tails the while they stood
& sprinkling thick their sides wi mud
Snuff the cool air now day is gone
& linger slow & idly on   390
To the pebbly fore to drink
& drop & rest upon its brink
Ruminating on their beds
Calm as the sky above their heads
The horse whose mouth is seldom still   395
Is up & cropping at his will
The moisting grass unteazd & free
In summer eves serenity
Uncheckt by flyes he grazes on
Right happy that the day is gone   400
Near leaving off to turn around
His stooping head to knap the wound
& tail that switchd his sides all day
Is quiet now the suns away
The cowboys as their herd plod on   405
Before them homward one by one
Grows happy as their toil grows short
& full of fancys restless sport
Oft struts along wi sinking day
Acting proud their soldier play   410
Wi peeld bark sash around each waist
& rush caps on each beaver placd
Stuck wi a head aches red cockade
& wooden swords & sticks displayd
For flags – thus march the evening troop   415
While some one strikes a whistle up
& others wi their dinner tins
The evenings falling quiet dins
Patting wi hollow sounding tums
Rude imitating fifes & drums   420
Calling their cows that plod before
Their army marching from the moor
& thus they act till met the town
Carless of laughs from passing clown
Where their dogs too tird for play   425
Loiter on their evening way

Oft rolling on the damping grass
Or stopping wi the milking lass
Waiting a chance the ways conseal
A mouth full from her pails to steal   430
Or dropping down to pick a bone
By hedger from his wallets thrown
Or found upon some greensward platt
Were hay folks at their dinner sat
Sweet comes the cows breath down the lane   435
Steaming the fragrance of the plain
As home they rock & bawling wait
Till boys run to unloose the gate
& from their milksheds all adry
Turn to the pump wi anxious eye   440
Were shoud the maids wi boys repair
To fill the dashing bucket there
They hurry spite of threatning clown
& kick the milkers bucket down
& horses oft wi eager stoop   445
Will bend adown to steal a sup
Watching a moments chance to win
& dip their eager noses in
As by they pass or set it down
To rest or chatter to a clown   450
& knats wi their small slender noise
Bother too the troubld boys
& teaze the cows that while she chides
Will kick & turn to lick their sides
& like so many hanting sprites   455
Will bite & weal the maid anights
Who dreams of love & sleeps so sound
As near to feel each little wound
Till waken by the morning sun
She wonders at the injury done   460
Thinking in fears simplicity
That faireys dreaded mistery
On her white bosom in the dark
Had been & left each blisterd mark
The fox begins his stunt odd bark   465
Down in its dew bed drops the lark

& on the heath amid the gorse
The night hawk sturts the feeding horse
That pricks his ear wi startling eye
& snorts to hear its trembling crye 470
The owlet leaves his ivy tree
& to its hive slow sails the bee
The mower seeks his cloaths & hides
His scythe home bent wi weary strides
& oer his shoulder swings his bag 475
Carr[y]ing in hand his empty cag
Hay makers on their homward way
To the fields will often stray
& mong the grain when no one sees
Nestle & fill their laps wi peas 480
Sheep scard wi tweenlight doubting eye
Leap the path & canter bye
Nipping wi moment stoops the plain
& turning qui[c]k to gaze again
Till silence upon eve awaits 485
& milkmaids cease to clap the gates
& homward to the town are gone
Wi whispering sweethearts chatting on
& shepherds homward tracks are past
& dogs rude barks are still at last 490
Then down they drop as suits their wills
Or nips the thyme on pismire hills
Were nought is seen but timid hares
That nights sweet welcome gladly shares
& shadows stooping as they stoop 495
Beside them when the moon gets up
Reviving wi the ruddy moon
The nightingale resumes his tune
What time the horsboy drives away
His loose teams from the toils of day 500
To crop the closes dewy blade
Were the haystacks fencd & made
Or on the commons bushy plain
To rest till the sun comes again
Whistling & bawling loud & long 505
The burthen of some drawling song

That grows more loud as eve grows late
Yet when he opes the clapping gate
He can t help turning in his joys
To look if his fear wakeing noise   510
Has raisd a mischief in the wind
& wakd a ghost to stalk behind
& when he s turnd them safe aground
& hookd the chain the gate around
Wi qui[c]ker speed he homward sings   515
& leaves them in the mushroom rings
Wi the dewdrunk dancing elves
To eat or rest as suits them selves
& as he hastes from labour done
An owlets whoop een makes him run   520
& bats shrill flickerings bobbing near
Turns his heart blood cold wi fear
& when at home wi partner ralph
He hugs himself to think he s safe
& tells his tale while others smile   525
Of all he thought & feard the while

A Village Evening

The black house bee hath ceasd to sing
& white nosd one wi out a sting
That boys will catch devoid of dread
Are in their little holes abed   530
& martins neath the mossey eves
Oft startld at the sparrow thieves
That in their house will often peep
Breaking their little weary sleep
& oft succeed when left alone   535
In making their clay huts their own
Were the cock sparrow on the scout
Watchs & keeps the owner out
The geese have left the home close moats
& at the yard gate clean their coats   540
Or neath their feathers tuck their heads
Asleep till driven to their sheds

The pigeon droves in whisking flight
Hurrying to their coats ere night
In coveys round the village meet 545
& in the dove coat holes retreat
Nor more about the wheaten grounds
The bird boys bell & clapper sounds
Returning wi the setting sun
His toil & shout & song is done 550
The shill bat wi its flittering mate
Starts thro the church vaults iron grate
Deaths daily visitors & all
He meets save slanting suns that fall
At eve as if they lovd to shed 555
Their daily memory oer the dead
Hodge neath the climbing elms that drop
Their branches oer a dove coat top
Hath milkd his cows & taken in
On yokes the reeking pales or tin 560
& been across the straw to chain
The hen roost wicket safe again
& done his yard rounds hunting eggs
& taen his hat from off the peggs
To scamper to the circling cross 565
To have a game at pitch & toss
& day boy hath his supper got
Of milk before twas hardly hot
Eager from toil to get away
& join the boys at taw to play 570
Neath black smiths cinder litterd shed
Till the hour to go to bed
Old gossips on their greensward bench
Sit were the hom bound milking wench
Will set her buckets down to rest 575
& be awhile their evening guest
To whom their box is held while she
Takes the smallest nips that be
That soon as snift begins to teaze
& makes her turn away to sneeze 580
While old dames say the sign is plain
That she will dream about her swain

& toss the cloaths from off her bed
& cautions her of roguish ned
Holding their hands agen their hips 585
To laugh as up she starts & trips
In quickend speed along the town
Bidding good night to passing clown
From the black smiths shop the swain
Jogs wi ploughshares laid again 590
& drops them by the stable shed
Were gears on pegs hang over head
Ready for driving boys to take
On fore horse when their toils awake
The kitchen wench wi face red hot 595
As blazing fire neath supper pot
Hath cleand her pails & pansions all
& set them le[an]ing by the wall
& twirld her whool mop clean again
& hung it on the pales to drain 600
Now by the maids requesting smile
The shepherd mounts the wood stack pile
Reard high against the orchard pails
& cause of thorns she oft bewails
Prickd hands & holes in sunday gown 605
He throws the smoothest faggot down
& hawks it in at her desire
Ready for the kitching fire
Beneath the elderns village shade
Oer her well curb leans the maid 610
To draw the brimming basket up
While passing boy to beg a sup
Will stop his roll or rocking cart
& the maidens gentle heart
Gives ready leave – the eager clown 615
Throws off his hat & stoops adown
Soaking his fill then hastens on
To catch his team already gone
Eager from toil to get release
& in the hay field feed at peace 620
The weary thresher leaves his barn
& emptys from his shoes the corn

That gatherd in them thro the day
& homward bends his weary way
The gardener he is sprinkling showers   625
From watering pans² on drooping flowers
& set away his hoe & spade
While goody neath the cottage shade
Sits wi a baskett tween her knees
Ready for supper shelling peas   630
& cobler chatting in the town
Hath put his window shutter down
& the knowing parish clerk
Feign to do his jobs ere dark
Hath timd the church clock to the sun   635
& wound it up for night & done
& turned the hugh kee in the door
Chatting his evening story oer
Up the street the servant maid
Runs wi her errands long delayd   640
& ere the door she enters in
She stops to right a loosend pin
& smooth wi hasty fingers down
The crumpling creases in her gown
Which Rogers oggles rudly made   645
For may games forfeit never paid
& seizd a kiss against her will
While plaing quoits upon the hill
Wi other shepherds laughing nigh
That made her shoy & hurry bye   650
The blacksmiths grizly toil is oer
& shut his hot shops branded door
Folding up his arms to start
& take at ease his evening quart
& farmer giles his business done   655
Wi face a very setting sun
Jogging home on dobbins back
From helping at the clover stack
The horse knows well nor trys to pass
The door were for his custom glass   660
He nightly from the saddle jumps
To slake his thirst or cheer the dumps

Leaving old dob his breath to catch
Wi bridle hanging at the latch
The shepherd too will often spare   665
A sixpence to be merry there
While the dog that trackd his feet
Adown the dusty printed street
Lies as one weary loath to roam
Agen the door to wait him home   670
While the taylors long day thirst
Is still unquenchd tho fit to burst
Whose been at truants merry play
From sheers & bodkin all the day
Still soaks the tankard reeling pipe   675
& scarce can stoop to light his pipe
The labourer sitting by his door
Happy that the day is oer
Is stooping downwards to unloose
His leathern baffles o[e]r his shoes   680
Making ready for his rest
Quickly to be the pillows guest
While on mothers lap wi in
The childern each their prayers begin
That taen from play are loath to go   685
& looking round repeating slow
Each prayer they stammer in delay
To gain from bed a longer stay
Goody hath set her spinning bye
Deafend by her chattering pye   690
That calls her up wi hungry rage
To put his supper in the cage
That done she sought a neighbours door
A minutes time to gossip oer
& neath her apron now tis night   695
Huddles for home³ her candle light
Hid from the wind – to burn an hour
As clouds wi threatend thunder lower
The mastiff from his kennel free
Is now unchaind at liberty   700
In readiness to put to rout
The thieves that night may bring about

Thus evening deepning to a close
Leaves toil & nature to repose

Appendix B

The Manuscripts of 'October'

Readers of *The Shepherd's Calendar* who are interested in exploring further the textual issues raised by Clare's manuscripts will find the example of 'October' particularly instructive. Lines contributing towards 'October' exist in four different manuscripts, followed by a transcript and then by the finally published version. These six versions, it should be emphasised, may not comprise the entire source material for the month, since some intermediate stages of drafting or editing may have been lost. But in chronological terms, the probable sequence of composition is:

Peterborough B5 a single page (p. 45) containing twenty lines drafted in pencil.

Peterborough A18 three pages (pp. 1–3) containing 104 lines, eight of which appear only in this version. The entire manuscript is marked 'done with'.

Peterborough A29 five pages (pp. 65–9) containing 108 lines, at first written as a fair copy, but later revised substantially. Single vertical lines through the text indicate the deletions, and single vertical lines at the left-hand margin indicate retentions, though this pointing is not consistently applied. A number of lines are written over with revised phrasing in darker ink. A tick against the title 'October' suggests that the alterations to this version have been dealt with.

Northampton 34 the opening eight lines, deleted, on the back of a letter from Clare to Taylor, 26 March 1826. Although deleted opening lines would generally suggest an early stage of drafting, the date of the letter suggests a much later placing in the chronology.

Peterborough B7 a transcript of four pages (pp. 61*a*, 62*a*, 63*a*, 65), with isolated corrections and gaps to indicate an indecipherable word.

SC the five pages of the published version (pp. 83–7).

These nineteen pages of source material raise three major editorial issues: the dating of the material, its transcription, and the collation of the different versions.

Dating[1]

If the sequencing of the manuscripts above is speculative, equally so is their dating. There is nothing in the first two manuscripts (B5 and A18) to narrow the date of drafting within the overall period 1822–6. The OET (SC [1996]) editors propose that the third manuscript in the sequence (Peterborough A29) is probably one of the two quarto exercise books that Taylor gave Clare in February 1822 (Taylor to Clare, 1 February 1822; Eg. 2246, fol. 11r), and that Hessey later commented upon in a letter to Clare of 3 November 1824 (Eg. 2246, fols. 405–6). February 1822 and November 1824 thus provide the outer dates for its contents. But it is clear that Clare was still working on 'October' some sixteen months later. On 18 March 1826, he writes to Taylor: '... "October" & "December" shall be with you directly tho I shall try to do the best I can with them' (*Letters*, p. 367). Eight days later, the opening lines are drafted and then deleted in a letter to Taylor (see Northampton 34 above). Moreover, there is no reference to 'October' earlier than Hessey's basic plan for the twelve months presented in his letter of 13 October 1823 (Eg. 2246, fols. 245–6). There, he proposes using for the month an already published poem ('The Last of Autumn'), strongly suggesting that the eventual poem 'October' had not at that stage been written. Overall, the evidence indicates a considerably later dating than that proposed in OET. Rather than February 1822–November 1824, a more likely dating is *after* October 1823–March 1826.

Transcription

The difficulties of deciphering Clare's manuscripts have long been recognised; and 'October' is no exception. Even when the vexed grammatical questions of variant spellings, absence of punctuation, and singular/plural conjunctions are set aside, Clare's basic handwriting remains difficult to read. His lettering is often cramped, making it hard to distinguish between 'sn', 'n', or 'm' at the beginning of a word, or 'ing' and 'y' at the end. His t's are often uncrossed, making them seem like l's. Lower case i's and j's are rarely dotted. An indeterminate flourish at the end of a word can signal a plural 's' or not. Words can be blotched, or smudged, or faded; and whole phrases and lines are sometimes erased by simply writing through them. Given this context, the skills of the OET editors (Eric Robinson, David Powell, and Paul Dawson) in actually deciphering Clare's words are outstanding. Indeed, it could well be the scrupulous accuracy of their transcription that will remain the most valuable achievement of this edition for future generations. In the OET text for 'October', only two over-written words in the entire manuscript sequence are judged indecipherable. All else is transcribed with meticulous care. Even these editorial skills, though, have not proved sufficient to prevent a substantial change of mind. Alterations that Robinson and Summerfield thought were in Taylor's hand, and which were therefore omitted from *SC* (1964), are now considered to be in Clare's, and are therefore, in *SC* (1996), restored. There could be few better illustrations of the difficulties presented by Clare's manuscripts than that his principal editors should not always have been able to recognise his own hand.

Collation of Versions

Given the accurate transcription of the words of 'October', the question arises of how to collate the six versions, especially in terms of their sequencing of lines. The table below may at first appear formidable; but it presents some easily understandable information. The 'consolidated text' is the final phrasing of each line in the manuscripts or printed text. Against these lines are their numbered position in the sources, which are presented in chronological order from left to right. Square brackets indicate a line that is written and then deleted.

Consolidated Text	B5	A18	A29	N34	B7	SC
Nature now spreads around in dreary hue	1	1	[1]		1	1
A pall to cover all that summer knew	2	2	[2]		2	2
Yet in the poets solitary way	3	3	[3]		3	3
Some pleasing objects for his praise delay	4	4	[4]		4	4
Somthing that makes him pause & turn again	5	5	[5]		5	5
As every trifle will his eye detain	6	6	[6]		6	6
The free horse rustling thro the stubble fields	7	7	[7]		7	7
& cows at lare in rushes half conscealed	8	8	[8]		8	8
With groups of restless sheep who feed their fill	9	9			9	9
Oer cleard fields rambling where so ere they will	10	10			10	10
The geese flock gabbling in the splashy fields	11	[11]			11	
& qua[c]king ducks in pondweeds half conseald	12	[12]			12	
Or seeking worms along the homclose sward	13	[13]			13	
Right glad of freedom from the prison yard	14	[14]			14	
While every cart rut dribbles its low tide	15	[15]			15	
& every hollow splashy sports provide	16	[16]			16	
The hedger stopping gaps amid the leaves	17	17			17	11
That oer his head in every color weaves	18	18			18	12
The milk maid stepping with a timid look	19	19			19	13
From stone to stone across the brimming brook	20	20			20	14
The cotter journeying wi his noisey swine	21	21			21	15
Along the wood ride were the brambles twine	22	22			22	16
Shaking from dinted cups the acorns brown	23	23			23	17
& from the hedges red awes dashing down	24	24			24	18
While nutters rustling in the yellow woods	25	25			25	19
Still scare the wild things from their solitudes	26	26			26	20
& squirrels secret toils oer winter dreams	27	[27]			27	
Picking the brown nuts from the yellow leams	28	[28]			28	
& hunters from the thickets avenue	29	29			29	21
In scarlet jackets startling on the view	30	30			30	22
Skiming a moment oer the russet plain	31	31			31	23
Then hiding in the colord woods again	32	32			32	24
The ploping guns sharp momentary shock	33	33			33	25
Which eccho bustles from her cave to mock	34	34			34	26
The inly pleasd tho solitary boy				107		27
Journeying & muttering oer his dreams of joy				108		28
Haunting the hedges for the wilding fruit				109		29
Of sloe or black berry just as fancys suit				110		30
The sticking groups in many a ragged set	35	[35]			35	
Brushing the woods their harmless loads to get	36	[36]			36	
& gipseys camps in some snug shelterd nook	37	[37]			37	31
Were old lane hedges like the pasture brook	38	[38]			38	32
Run crooking as they will by wood & dell	39	39			39	33
In such lone spots these wild wood roamers dwell	40	40			40	34
On commons were no farmers claims appear	41	[41]			41	

Consolidated Text	B5	A18	A29	N34	B7	SC
Nor tyrant justice rides to interfere		42	[42]		42	
Such the abodes neath hedge or spreading oak		43	43		43	35
& but discovered by its curling smoak		44	44		44	36
Puffing & peeping up as wills the breeze		45	45		45	37
Between the branches of the colord trees		46	46		46	38
Such are the pictures that october yields		47	47		47	39
To please the poet as he walks the fields		48	48		48	40
While nature like fair woman in decay			69			41
Which pale consumption hourly wastes away			70			42
Upon her waining features pale & chill			71			43
Wears dreams of beauty that seem lovely still			72			44
Among the heath furze still delights to dwell			73			45
Quaking as if with cold the harvest bell			74			46
The mushroom buttons each moist morning brings		49	75		49	47
Like spots of snow in the green tawney rings		50	76		50	48
& fuzz balls swelld like bladders in the grass		51	77		51	
Which oft the merry laughing milking lass		52	78		52	
Will stoop to gather in her sportive airs		53	79		53	
& slive in mimicked fondness unawares		54	80		54	
To smut the brown cheek of the teasing swain		55	81		55	
With the black powder which their balls contain		56	82		56	
Who feigns offence at first that love may speed			83			
Then claims a kiss to recompence the deed			84			
The singing maid in fancy ever gay	1	85	[49]		57	
Loitering along the mornings dripping way	2	86	[50]		58	
With wicker basket swinging on her arm	3	87	[51]		59	
Searching the hedges of home close or farm	4	88	[52]		60	
Where brashy eldern trees to autumn fade	5	89	[53]		61	49
Wild shines each hedge in autumns gay parade	6	90	[54]		62	50
The glossy berrys picturesquely weaves	7	91	[55]		63	51
Their swathy bunches mid the yellow leaves	8	92	[56]		64	52
Where the pert sparrow stains his little bill	9	93	[57]		65	53
& tutling robin picks his meals at will	10	94	[58]		66	54
Black ripening to the wan suns misty ray	11	95	[59]		67	
Here the industrous hus wives wend their way	12	96	[60]		68	
Pulling the brittle branches carefull down	13	97	[61]		69	
& hawking loads of berrys to the town	14	98	[62]		70	
While village dames as they get ripe & fine	15	99	[63]		71	55
Repair to pluck them for their 'eldern wine'	16	100	[64]		72	56
That bottld up becomes a rousing charm	17	101	65		73	57
To kindle winters icy bosom warm	18	102	66		74	58
That wi its merry partner nut brown beer	19	103	67		75	59
Makes up the peasants christmass keeping cheer	20	104	68		76	60
Like to a painted map the landscape lies;						61

Consolidated Text

	B5	A18	A29	N34	B7	SC
And wild above, shine the cloud-thronged skies,						62
The flying clouds urged on in swiftest pace	57	85			77	63
Like living things as if they runned a race	58	86			78	64
The winds that oer each coming tempest broods		87				65
Waking like spirits in their startling moods		88				66
Fluttering the sear leaves on the blackning lea	59	89			79	67
That litters under every fading tree	60	90			80	68
& pausing oft as falls the patting rain	61	91			81	69
Then gathering strength & twirling them again	62	92			82	70
Till drops the sudden calm:– the hurried mill						71
Is stopt at once, and every noise is still						72
The startld stockdove hurried wizzing bye	63	[93]			83	
As the still hawk hangs oer him in the sky	64	[94]			84	
Crows from the oak trees quawking as they spring	65	95			85	73
Dashing the acorns down wi beating wing	66	96			86	74
Waking the woodlands sleep in noises low	67	97			87	75
Patting the crimpt brakes withering brown below	68	98			88	76
The starnel crowds that dim the muddy light	69	99			89	77
& puddock circling round its lazy flight	70	100			90	78
Round the wild sweeing wood in motion slow	71	101			91	79
Before it perches on the oaks below	72	102			92	80
& hugh black beetles revelling alone	[73]	103			93	81
In the dull evening with their heavy drone	[74]	104			94	82
Buzzing from barn door straw & hovel sides	[75]	105			95	
Were fodder cattle from the night abides	[76]	106			96	
These pictures linger thro the shortning day		107			97	83
& cheer the lone bards mellancholy way		108			98	84
Till surly Winter comes with biting breath,						85
And strips the woods, and numbs the scene with death;					86	
Then all is still o'er wood and field and plain,						87
As nought had been, and nought would be again.						88

[additional lines found in only one manuscript]

	B5
The pulp hips reddening on the bowing briar	77
& sloes blue clusters which the boys admire	78
In each bush border by close sides are seen	79
& narrow lanes were rushes linger green	80
In the old fences round the thorns tannd bough	81
The tangling brambles hang their berrys now	82
Delighting childen who will leave their play	83
& dithering seek them on the sabbath day	84

What a study of this table soon reveals is the complexity of the evolution between the different stages of drafting. Over twenty lines, for example, appear in an early draft, then disappear from a later, then reappear in the transcript, only to disappear again from the printed text. Another eight lines appear in one manuscript only, and nowhere else. 'Runs' of lines can be juxtaposed against each other differently. Although all drafts begin similarly, there are at least three different conclusions. Most remarkably, perhaps, there are eight lines that appear *only in the published text*, without any supporting manuscript authority. Not only do the OET editors appear to accept that these lines are Clare's (rather than Taylor's), but they actually print them unpunctuated and with ampersands, as if their provenance is actually Clare's manuscripts, rather than the published version only.

These difficulties of dating, transcription, and collation may help to explain why Clare's texts – of 'October', of *The Shepherd's Calendar* in general, and of much else in his work – have been so fiercely debated. But although the contest between different schools of editing has been vigorous, even bitter, it has conferred one inestimable benefit. The scholarly ghost of the 'definitive edition' has been laid for ever to rest. No such edition of 'October', or of *The Shepherd's Calendar*, will ever exist. What will exist is the saving pluralism of different editorial views and positions, as they are presented, then challenged, then reassessed, then re-presented differently. In so far as this book contributes towards that pluralism, it will have more than fulfilled its purpose.

NOTES

Introduction

1 Taylor's first meeting with Clare took place on 13 November 1819, and he subsequently wrote on 30 November and 21 January 1820 with the detailed suggestions indicated above (Northampton MS 44, and British Library, Egerton MS 2245, fols. 25r–6v [hereafter cited as 'Eg.']).

2 Taylor seems to have anticipated this question as early as August 1823, when he proposed adding '& other Poems' to the general title, in order to 'take in such at the End as would not come well in under the Months' (Eg. 2246, fol. 228v). A number of such pieces (for example, 'To the Cowslip', 'The Dream', 'Antiquity', 'Poesy') were eventually placed at the end of the 1827 volume, in a section simply entitled 'Poems'. However, such a characterisation and position in the text, clearly separated from the title-poem, and also from the 'Village Stories', served only to highlight the differences between 'description', 'narrative', and 'other poems', that remained to the end.

3 4 March 1826. Eg. 2247, fol. 152v.

4 The view was first fully propounded by Eric Robinson and Geoffrey Summerfield in 'John Taylor's Editing of Clare's *The Shepherd's Calendar*', *Review of English Studies*, n.s. 14 (November 1963), and then in their introduction to *The Shepherd's Calendar* (Oxford: Oxford University Press, 1964). Since that time, the criticism of Taylor has been rehearsed in a number of articles and editions, and not only by its original proponents. The most recent (Alan Vardy, *John Clare, Politics and Poetry* [Basingstoke: Palgrave Macmillan, 2003]) is also the strongest. The qualifying view first presented in my *A Publisher and his Circle: The Life and Work of John Taylor, Keats's Publisher*, (London: Routledge & Kegan Paul, 1972), has been supported more recently in Zachery Leader, 'John Taylor and the Poems of Clare', in his *Revision and Romantic Authorship* (Oxford: Clarendon Press, 1996); in Roger Sales, *John Clare: A Literary Life* (Basingstoke: Palgrave, 2002); and in Jonathan Bate, *John Clare: A Biography* (London: Picador, 2003).

5 *Letters*, pp. 140, 146, 288, 364, 365, 382, respectively.

6   Taylor delegated the transcription of some of the manuscripts to Harry Stoe Van Dyk and to Fleetwood, an employee of the firm. But their efforts left a good deal to be desired. As Taylor wrote to Clare on 28 January 1826, 'I can find *no one* here who can perform the Task besides myself. Copying it therefore is a Farce for not three words in a Line on the Average are put down right, & the Number omitted, by those whom I have got to transcribe it, are so great, that it is easier for me at once to sit down & write it fairly out myself.' (Eg. 2247, fols. 132v–133r).

7   See *Letters*, pp. 294, 292.

8   For example, advance copies of *The Shepherd's Calendar* were in fact available, and six were sent to Clare, at the end of November 1826 (Eg. 2247, fol. 230). But Peter De Wint's frontispiece drawing, which went through two versions, and especially the engraving of it, occasioned further delay. On 19 February 1827, Taylor wrote to Clare that the drawing had been 'some Time at the Engraver's, by whom it was promised to be finished in about a Week from this Time.–' (Eg. 2247, fol. 265r). But the engraver wanted to take his time and complete the plate 'in a very superior Manner', and also met with an unspecified 'acccident' (Eg. 2247, fol. 274r). The result was that the book with its prefatory engraving was not actually published until the end of April 1827.

9   Hessey importantly suggested both a general and a detailed plan. Overall, the poem should delineate 'the face of Nature, the operations of the husbandman, the amusements, festivals, superstitions, customs &c of the Country, and little stories introduced to illustrate these more accurately and to fix an Interest on them.' He then followed this general outline with detailed possibilities for each of the twelve months:

January	– New Year's Day – Winter Sports – Skating &c –
February	– Valentine's Day – a good subject for a Love story
March	First approach of Spring
April	– The Poem of Spring already written, with the addition of some little Story
May	– The Day Dream
June	Haymaking – an abundant theme for Stories
July	– Sheep shearing – the same
August	– Harvest beginning – last of Summer
September	– Harvest Home – a capital Subject – describe a real Scene

October	– the last of Autumn – Field Sports – Story
November	– Dismal feelings on the Approach of Winter Pathetic Story
December	– Frost, Snow, Christmas Gambols Winter Sports – Miseries of the very poor – Story –

(Eg. 2246, fols. 245v–246r. 13 October 1823)

10 Taylor particularly praised the following section, which he quoted in its entirety:

> Noon gathers wi its blistering breath
> Around & day dyes still as death
> The breeze is stopt the lazy bough
> Hath not a leaf that dances now
> The totter grass upon the hill
> & spiders threads is hanging still
> The feathers dropt from morehens wings
> Upon the waters surface clings
> As stedfast & as heavy seem
> As stones beneath them in the stream
> Hawkweed & groundsels fairey downs
> Unruffld keep their seeding crowns
> & in the oven heated air
> Not one light thing is floating there
> Save that to the earnest eye
> The restless heat swims twittering bye

This almost impressionistic description of a stultifying noonday heat is unquestionably one of the finest sections in the month, and indeed in the whole poem. Its verbal tautness, and the contribution of each natural detail to the larger imaginative centre of blistering heat, make for a resonant evocation. For a further discussion of these lines, see my *A Publisher and his Circle*, pp. 116–19.

11 It is easy to exaggerate Clare's idiosyncracies in spelling and punctuation, however, as Bob Heyes points out to me in a letter of October 2004. Standardisation of English had been only partially achieved in the early nineteenth century; and variations in grammar, even among literate and educated members of society, were still considerable.

12 This example was first discussed in my *A Publisher and his Circle*, pp. 113–15, and is subsequently taken up by Leader (n. 4 above).

13 See n. 4 above.

14 28 January 1826. Eg. 2247, fol. 133.

15 See n. 3 above.

16 I explore the issues involved in the dating of the months in 'The Dating of Clare's *The Shepherd's Calendar*', *John Clare Society Journal*, no. 25 (July 2006), 65–77.

17 Clare to De Wint, 14 October 1827. *Letters*, pp. 399–400.

18 *The Literary Chronicle* (no. 441, 674–5) concluded that for 'accurate pictures of rural scenery, in depth of feeling, and originality of observation', Clare was 'inferior to no poet of the day.' *The Eclectic Review* (n.s. xxvii, 509–21), in a lengthy review by Josiah Conder, found 'unequivocal signs of intellectual growth, an improved taste, and an enriched mind. This progressive improvement is one of the surest indications of a mind endowed with the vigorous stamina of genius.'

19 An unsigned notice in the *London Weekly Review* for 9 June 1827 (i, 7) found some of the phraseology 'unintelligible', and an unsigned review in the *Monthly Review* for the same month objected to 'the use of vulgar epithets, or expressions; not provincialisms merely, but absolute specimens of *patois*, and whose *expressive* qualities by no means atone for their inelegance … they are the progeny of a vicious taste, that cannot be too sparingly indulged in, nor too soon abandoned altogether.' (v, 277).

20 See Taylor's account of 16 January 1826, reporting the collapse of Hurst Robinson, Constable, and 'several smaller Houses' (*A Publisher and his Circle*, p. 184).

21 Cited in Amy Cruse, *The Englishman and his Books in the Early Nineteenth Century* (London: George Harrap, 1930, p. 148).

22 No. 212, 19 November 1831, p. 755.

23 See *John Clare By Himself*, ed. Eric Robinson and David Powell (Ashington and Manchester: Mid-Northumberland Arts Group and Carcanet Press, 1996), pp. 156–8.

24 See, for instance, Jane Welsh's report to Thomas Carlyle, 'Byron is dead! I was told it all at once in a roomful of people. My God, if they had said that the sun or the moon had gone out of the heavens, it could not have struck me with the idea of a more awful and dreary blank in the creation.' Quoted in Leslie Marchand, *Byron: A Portrait* (London: John Murray, 1971), pp. 467–8.

25 *England and the English*, Book iv, ch. 2.

26 See *John Clare: Poems of the Middle Period 1822–1837*, 5 vols., ed. Eric Robinson, David Powell and P.M.S. Dawson (Oxford: Clarendon

Press, 1996–2003), v, pp. 558–67.

27 An extrapolation from the statement in *SC* (1993), ix, that over 5,000 copies of the 1964 edition were sold between 1964 and 1993.

28 *Studies in Human Time*, trans. Elliott Coleman (Baltimore and London: Johns Hopkins University Press, 1956), pp. 23–4.

Dedication and Preface

1 Clare's draft dedication occurs in a letter to Taylor of mid-July 1826 (Northampton MS 32, fol. 92. *Letters*, p. 382).

2 Clare's 'final' draft preface, with his own deletions, builds upon an earlier, shorter version. See *Poems of the Middle Period* (n. 26 above) v, pp. 554–7.

The Shepherd's Calendar

1 There could be no more dramatic illustration of the textual questions raised by *The Shepherd's Calendar* than the very first word – indeed, the very first letter – of the poem. Having adopted the reading 'Withering' in all their editions up to 1996, the OET editors now read 'Dithering'. 'Withering' first appears in a fair copy (MS B3) made by one of Taylor's amanuenses, presumably because 'Dithering' was either mis-read or not understood in its dialect sense of 'trembling with cold'.

2 The two parts of Clare's evocation of January, 'A Winters Day' and 'A Cottage Evening', were eventually elided into a single section.

3 Opposite this title, Clare's friend Mrs Emmerson writes in Peterborough MS A29: 'The Description / of the Fairies / may perhaps / do – the / rest not'. She confirms the preference by writing 'See / from / this / place / to / the / End' against ll. 114–22.

4 A convoluted squiggle at the end of this line and the next (MS A29) suggests that Clare may have intended them to conclude 'treads' and 'threads', even though they then present a plural noun/singular verb combination.

5 Although obviously a slip of the pen, Clare clearly writes 'sleeps' in MS A29.

6 In the margin of MS A29, opposite this line, Mrs Emmerson writes 'Very good / from here'.

7 In MS A29, Taylor pencils in a number of emendations and clarifications of words, all of which are carried over into the published version of 'February' and the recto-page readings here. The verso-page readings, of course, remain Clare's manuscript before emendation. The larger question of the reorganisation of stanzas for this month is discussed in the Introduction, pp. xiv–xvi, above.

8 The fourth word in this line has occasioned considerable debate, with suggested readings of 'merry' and 'morning', as well as 'mourning'. As is noted in *SC* (1996), 32, white was a colour of mourning in Clare's day, and probably makes best sense in the context of the 'stiffening stream…numb[ed] into ice' and the 'icicles that fret at noon'.

9 In two of the three extant manuscripts of 'April' (Peterborough MS D7 and Pforzheimer Library, Misc. MS 198), the stanzas are numbered, though their sequencing is differently arranged.

10 Adherence to the rhyme of 'gales' seems to have led to the plural 'pales', even though the grammatical sense is clearly 'turning *pale*'.

11 In two of the manuscripts, Clare writes a row of seven crosses between ll.32/33, and again between 40/41 and 88/89, as if to indicate an omitted stanza or lines.

12 In MS A29, the title actually reads 'June – Sheepsheering &c'. The pencilled emendations in this manuscript are Taylor's, sometimes clarifying Clare's script, sometimes altering it. As with n. 7 above, the verso-page readings here remain Clare's manuscript before Taylor's emendations.

13 Taylor's criticism of the length and quality of the first version of 'July', to which Clare responded, is discussed in the Introduction, pp. xii, xviii above. Clare's second version is presented here since, whatever the merits of each side in the argument, it represents the 'final' manuscript version of the month. The 704 lines of July I are presented in Appendix A above.

14 In MS B6, Clare actually writes 'saxton castles'.

15 In MS B6, Clare actually writes 'taunts', rather than 'taints'.

16 In MS A20, immediately before the title, Clare writes: '"I leave them as a father does his son" Keats Feb: 1824'.

17 The draft manuscripts of 'October' present some of the most complicated textual problems in the entire poem, and are discussed in Appendix B above.

18 This last word of the line clearly reads 'farms', even though Clare presumably intended the singular form, to accord with 'arm'.

19 This and the following line occur only in the published version, and in none of the extant manuscripts.

20 This and the following line occur only in the published version, and in none of the extant manuscripts.

21 This and the following three lines occur only in the published version, and in none of the extant manuscripts.

22 As with 'October' (see Appendix B and n. 17 above), the sequencing of stanzas in 'November' raises some substantial questions. The ordering of verses in *SC* (1996) is, as with 'October', a collation of various sources (chiefly, 1827 published version, MSS A20, A18 and B3), rather than the expression of a single manuscript sequence. The manuscripts differ both in their ordering of stanzas, and in their retentions and omissions. Towards the end of the sequence in A20, Clare writes significantly: 'I have sent this rough book tis all I have got / of the Calender here & if I shoud get better / you may send me it back to finish if not you must / make the best of it…'.

23 I follow *SC* (1996) here in supplying what is otherwise an uncompleted stanza with the missing line from the same stanza in 'The Summer Gone', l. 54. A number of lines in 'The Summer Gone' overlap with those in 'November' (see *SC* [1996], 144).

24 The addition of a third rhyming line in ll. 166–8 results in this stanza having ten lines, rather than the obligatory nine.

Appendix A

1 The manuscript here clearly reads 'follow fields', though this is obviously a slip of the pen for 'fallow fields'.

2 The manuscript here clearly reads 'watering pans', though this may be a slip of the pen for 'watering cans'.

3 *SC* (1996) supplies a comma after 'huddles for home', though there is none in MS A20.

Appendix B

1 The subject of the period of composition for each of the months, 'October' included, is discussed further in my 'The Dating of Clare's *The Shepherd's Calendar*', *John Clare Society Journal*, no. 25, July 2006, pp. 65–77.

SOURCES, ABBREVIATIONS AND
FURTHER READING

Manuscripts

The major manuscript sources for *The Shepherd's Calendar* are Peterborough Museum MSS A18, A19, A20, A29, A30, A31, B3, B6, D7, supplemented by the letters contained in Northampton Public Library MS 32. The standard bibliographies for these two collections are Margaret Grainger, *A Descriptive Catalogue of the John Clare Collection in Peterborough Museum and Art Gallery* (Peterborough: printed for the Earl Fitzwilliam, 1973); and [David Powell], *Catalogue of the John Clare Collection in the Northampton Public Library* (Northampton: Northampton Public Library, 1964). For readers interested in examining Clare's actual manuscripts, all of this material is readily available on microfilm (Microform Academic Publishers, Wakefield). Additional material in the United States is to be found in the Pforzheimer Collection (Misc. MS 198) of the New York Public Library. The Egerton MSS 2245–9 in the British Library contain many invaluable letters *to* Clare from Taylor, Hessey, Mrs Emmerson, and others.

Published Editions

The major editions of the poem (excluding collections or anthologies that contain extracts only) are:

SC (1827)	*The Shepherd's Calendar; with Village Stories and other Poems*. London: pub. for John Taylor by James Duncan, 1827. [Facsimile of this edition, with introduction by Jonathan Wordsworth, Woodstock Books: Oxford and New York, 1991].
SC (1935)	*The Poems of John Clare*, ed. J.W. Tibble, 2 vols. London and New York: Dent and Dutton, 1935. Vol. 1, pp. 287–341.
SC (1964)	*The Shepherd's Calendar*, ed. Eric Robinson and Geoffrey Summerfield. London: Oxford University

	Press, 1964 [re-issued in paperback form, 1973].
SC (1993)	rev. 2nd. edition of the above, ed. Eric Robinson, Geoffrey Summerfield, and David Powell. Oxford: Oxford University Press, 1993.
SC (1996), OET	*Poems of the Middle Period 1822–1837*, ed. Eric Robinson, David Powell, and P.M.S. Dawson, 5 vols. Oxford: Clarendon Press (Oxford English Texts), 1996. Vol. 1, pp. 1–162.

Invaluable contextual material is to be found in:

| *CH* | *Clare: The Critical Heritage*, ed. Mark Storey. London: Routledge & Kegan Paul, 1972. |
| *Letters* | *Letters of John Clare*, ed. Mark Storey. Oxford: Clarendon Press, 1985. |

Critical Reading

Few, if any, books on Clare fail to examine selected aspects of *The Shepherd's Calendar*, however briefly. But for critical discussions specifically focused upon the poem, and of at least article- or chapter-length, the following material is useful:

Barrell, John   *The Idea of Landscape and the Sense of Place 1730–1840: An Approach to the Poetry of John Clare*. Cambridge: Cambridge University Press, 1972 [esp. pp. 169–73].

Bate, Jonathan   *John Clare: A Biography*. Basingstoke and Oxford: Picador, 2003 [esp. pp. 295–317].

Chilcott, Tim   *A Publisher and his Circle: The Life and Work of John Taylor, Keats's Publisher*. London: Routledge & Kegan Paul, 1972 [esp. pp. 103–23].

—— *'A Real World & Doubting Mind': A Critical Study of the Poetry of John Clare*. Pickering: Hull University Press, 1985 [pp. 34–68].

—— 'The Dating of Clare's *The Shepherd's Calendar*', *John Clare Society Journal*, no. 25, July 2006, pp. 65–77.

Gorji, Mina   'Clare's "Merry England"', *John Clare Society Journal*, no. 24, July 2005, pp. 5–24.

Howard, William   *John Clare*. Boston, MA: Twayne Publishers, 1981 [pp. 73–82].

Jack, Ian   'Poems of John Clare's Sanity', in *Some British Romantics*, ed. James V. Logan, John E. Jordan and Northrop Frye. Columbus, OH: Ohio State University Press, 1966 [esp. pp. 207–22].

Leader, Zachery   'John Taylor and the Poems of Clare', in his *Revision and Romantic Authorship*. Oxford: Clarendon Press, 1996, pp. 206–61.

Lucas, John   *John Clare*. Plymouth: Northcote House, 1994 [pp. 49–53].

Robinson, Eric, and Geoffrey Summerfield   'John Taylor's Editing of Clare's *The Shepherd's Calendar*', *Review of English Studies*, n.s. xiv, no. 56, 1963, pp. 359–69.

Robinson, Eric, David Powell and P.M.S. Dawson (eds.)   *John Clare: Cottage Tales*. Ashington and Manchester: Mid-Northumberland Arts Group and Carcanet Press, 1993 [pp. xvii–xxxiii].

Sales, Roger   *John Clare: A Literary Life*. Basingstoke: Palgrave, 2002 [esp. pp. 66–75].

Storey, Mark   *The Poetry of John Clare: A Critical Introduction*. London: Macmillan, 1974 [pp. 50–113].

Todd, Janet M.   *In Adam's Garden: A Study of John Clare's Pre-Asylum Poetry*. Gainesville, FL: University of Florida (Humanities Monograph no. 39), 1973 [pp. 17–27].

Vardy, Alan   *John Clare, Politics and Poetry*. Basingstoke: Palgrave, 2003 [esp. pp. 4–9, 137–49].

Links

The two best guides to current and future explorations of *The Shepherd's Calendar* are the *John Clare Society Journal* (1982–), ed. John Goodridge; and the Clare website, ed. Simon Kövesi, at http://www.johnclare.info. Both sources are widely recognised for their excellence.

INDEX